For Julia,
just because she's cool.

Small Business Ideas: 400 Latest & Greatest
Small Business Ideas - The World's Largest Source of
The Latest & Greatest Successful Small Business Ideas From Around The
World; New Small Business Ideas, Small Business Management, Small
Business Start-Ups and New Ventures; Real Businesses & Real Entrepreneurs
Making Real Money in Successful Small Businesses.
2008/09 International Edition.

Edited by Terry Kyle

ISBN 978-0-9558989-0-7

TheWorldsBiggestBooks.com
is located in:

Malden Road
Borehamwood WD6 1BN
United Kingdom.

© TheWorldsBiggestBooks.com

~
So, Who Is This Book For?
~

O k, let's get started. First question: who on earth is this reference book intended for? Well, mainly it is:

(1) Readers frustrated with their conventional 9-5 employment and are seeking a dramatic 'life change' by opening their own business in order to take greater control of their own destiny. Yet how would such a person know what great new small businesses are now opening up around the world? In short, this book presents a type of 'snapshot' of the best, newest and most interesting small businesses that have recently opened up across the globe. Aspiring small business entrepreneurs should also know about the best small businesses and *products* – on which an outstanding business can be built - from the last couple of years along with the best 'blue-chip' small businesses of all time that should always be considered.

This book also offers some of the best small business advice on how to make sure that an entrepreneur's first small business is not their last – though other books out there go into this side of small business in much more detail. Reading and adhering to the chapter on *Small Business 'Micro-Mastery'* on Page 267 will also give you every chance of 'making it' in small business.

It should also be pointed out that this book does not attempt any form of in-depth analysis on the businesses listed as many other books already focus on specific small business types.

(2) Readers who are already active small business entrepreneurs interested in applying new developments and products in the world of small business to their existing ventures (many small businesses consist of multiple revenue streams). These entrepreneurs may be seeking to diversify their business or shift their entire focus to a dynamic new product or small business development.

(3) Innovation-hungry entrepreneurs *within* larger businesses who can see the obvious benefit of applying some of these new approaches or products in their organization. Smart entrepreneurs know that the world of business doesn't stand still and neither should they; and,

(4) Sacked workers who have unexpectedly found themselves thrown on the corporate scrap-heap after decades of service and whose age - scandalously - is proving a negative factor in finding new conventional employment.

* * * * *

Hopefully, reading about the wonderful, brilliant and occasionally strange new small businesses that have been collated in this research text will illustrate the importance of these particular axioms included in *The Best Quotes Of All Time About Business* section on Page 63:

"Knowledge is important. The ability to act is critical."

"It's not *what* you sell that matters.
It's *how* (well) you sell it."

'Business is about converting prospects into customers.
Everything else is secondary.'

'The success of every single business in the world hinges on how well it *communicates* - with clients, potential clients, suppliers, stakeholders, within itself and with the world.'

~

~
About
The
Editor.

~

T erry Kyle's professional background includes screenwriting, playwriting, PR, broadcast journalism and copywriting for some of the world's largest blue-chip companies.

While completing a medal-winning BA at Griffith University in Brisbane in 1994, Terry wrote and directed a feature-length science-fiction telemovie, *Terrain*, a science-fiction thriller, which was subsequently screened several times by the Nine Network. Nine were Australia's #1 broadcaster then, though they slipped to #2 after screening *Terrain* and have never recovered.

Terry holds a Masters degree in Teaching Drama & English from the University of Sydney. In 2004, he appeared as Maloy in a satirical digital feature entitled *Wango & Maloy* which he co-wrote and co-produced.

During the 1990s, he worked as a copywriter and creative director in 'through-the-line' marketing and advertising agencies such as Chapman & Lester and MarketSMART on clients like Pepsi, Kellogg's, Thomas Cook, Commonwealth Bank and AIS in Thailand.

He has been involved in numerous business ventures in Australia over the past 20 years and currently resides in North London, England.

Apart from his cheeky girlfriend, Terry's main loves in life are Salsa, Japanese sports cars, marinated tofu, Kurt Vonnegut, acoustic folk-rock like The Church, paisley shirts, Bruce Dawe's poetry, Thailand, golden retrievers, Canada's Rocky Mountains, John Pilger's documentaries, Kyokushin karate and seahorses.

He is the founding editor of TheWorldsBiggestBooks.com and, as you read this, is busy working on his beloved yellow laptop on the next 'World's Biggest Book of *Something*'.

~

~

Introduction.

~

Welcome to *400 Latest & Greatest Small Business Ideas*. If you are reading this book, then you clearly hold the desire to become the mistress or master of your own professional destiny - a passionate desire that more and more individuals are discovering in an age of corporate downsizing, blatant age discrimination and salary expectations of 60-80+ hours of work a week.

Enough! It's time to 'do the math'.

It's time to do the research, time to count the pennies, time to re-structure your life and time to take the first steps on *your* small business journey. And that is precisely what this book attempts to help you to do - successfully step into that bigger world.

But what you haven't been told about small business by our corporation overlords is that it *doesn't* have to be financially risky and *doesn't* have to break you forever if it fails.

That sort of talk is out there to stop the 'herd' from taking over the farm. The same sort of 'wisdom' keeps people in 'cheap', 'easy' credit card deals for life. Learning to spot such social myths and lies that seek to economically enslave us is one vitally important skill to develop on your small business journey.

In small business, we work smart. In a way, it's kind of *guerrilla* business - fast, mobile, clever and tactically sophisticated; attributes that big corporations simply fall down on all the time.

Plus, don't forget that Microsoft and Apple Computers were once garage operations too! However, big does not necessarily mean better. The focus should always be on quality of life. The quality of *your* life - something that no other person on the planet is responsible for.

Hopefully, as you read this book, you will understand that the concepts talked about here are not restricted to business but are actually about building a *whole* life, a great life - provided you have the courage and determination to go after that life! So let's put on the seat belt and buckle up for the exhilarating, demanding and ultimately rewarding journey into your own small business venture (perhaps the first of many).

Though this book includes 400+ great and new small business ideas from around the world, smart entrepreneurs are *always* looking for new opportunities and new approaches through their own lateral thinking.

Having this mental 'detective' permanently 'switched on' will have an enormous effect on your small business success. But - and in life there is so often a 'but' - all of the most brilliant ideas, knowledge, secrets and approaches in the world are worth absolutely nothing without one thing:

the will to Act.

Remember, this book does not attempt any form of in-depth analysis on the listed businesses here as many other books focus on specific small business types e.g. running a vending machine business (an excellent type of starting small business, by the way).

The intention here is to give you a massively broad - but not deep - 'snapshot' of the best small business innovation in the world today and from the last couple of years. When you find a business or small business*es* that appeal, you can *then* purchase other reference works that go into that particular type of business in much more detail.

Your first step however, would be to thoroughly 'deconstruct' the commercial model of an appealing small business/es that you have identified here.

Rock on.
Terry Kyle
Managing Editor,
TheWorldsBiggestBooks.com

~
Table
of
Contents.

~

~ Table of Contents ~

~

~

1.
The Biggest Mistakes That Small Business Entrepreneurs Make.

~

A mong the worst mistakes that budding small business entrepreneurs make include these clangers - oops!:

1. Committing to high overheads based on *potential* rather than *actual* business. Shop or office leases, car leases, computer equipment purchases, business cards, glossy flyers, huge Yellow Pages' ads, staff salaries, letterheads, press advertising - they all add up. Especially for a new business that *will* take some time to establish. All businesses do. If a healthy, established small business is only earning in the vicinity of 20% net profit on turnover, how can such expenses be afforded? Especially *without* steady income coming in. They can't without borrowing usually - another business expense in terms of interest charges - and such ventures are already building momentum *against* their efforts. Momentum is everything - in business and in life. Businesses *must* grow organically if they are to survive. Expenditure *must* work as a proportion of income. This may lack 'sizzle' and may not be 'glamorous' but there's nothing sexy about bankruptcy.

2. Not offering anything new in the way of a product or service. Consumer buying patterns are based on certain recurrent factors: location (gas stations, 7-11s); price (Wal-Mart); familiarity/location (doctor/accountant); ease of purchase (TV infomercials); financing attractiveness (cars); brand/product/image loyalty (Nike). Obviously there are overlaps in each of these areas but for your new business, there *must* be one (or more) of the above reasons working for you: e.g. yours is the *only/coolest/fastest* internet café in the area.

In short, there *must* be a very clear, tangible reason why a consumer or client would buy *your* product or service and *not* someone else's. Rather than thinking, 'if I build it, they will come', think, 'if I build it intelligently and low-cost/no-cost market the hell out of it, they will come.' See Page 60 for precisely how to market a new small business on a low-cost/no-cost basis.

Even with that differentiation, consumers need some *time* to discover the 'killer attribute' through marketing action. Potential buyers do not immediately jump at something new. It takes time for the message to sink in and critical mass to build up. When it does though, it is pretty cool and makes the sacrifices and hard work worthwhile.

3. **Being Impatient**. Many small business newbies thus have this naïve, aforementioned 'I will build it and they will come' mentality. These newbies - which we all were once - are then profoundly disappointed when 'they' inevitably don't come. Or at least not in sufficient numbers. The only kinds of business where this instant-success dynamic *might* happen are new retail ventures in incredibly busy locations. The bad news is that such ventures usually require a *lot* of start-up capital.

Building a business takes time. In fact, smart operators start up their new small business *before* leaving their other job. This can be physically demanding BUT makes the economic transition a much easier one. Be patient with your new business but keep learning and modifying your operation - even the name of your business/product/service may need fine-tuning.

4. **Lack of marketing oomph.** In today's ultra-cluttered marketing world, you have to work hard to get your message through. Across countless small business ventures, I have always found small, local newspapers (not the big, expensive city-wide ones) marvellously cost effective.

Here's something else that the advertising industry - where I used to work as a Creative Director - doesn't want you to find out: *classifieds* in those same papers perform much better than more expensive, graphics-intensive display ads! Crazy, huh? Embracing the 'counter-intuitive' reality of the world is vitally important if a small business is going to survive and succeed.

Depending on your business, I can't recommend this marketing option highly enough among the many you will use.

It's cheap, has impact and real flexibility - change your ad every week if need be e.g. new specials, new offers. Big companies can only dream of this kind of flexibility as they're addicted to large, over-produced and massively over-priced glossy campaigns that 'brand-build' i.e. squander millions pointlessly.

Simply being 'open for business' has very little marketing oomph. You must work tirelessly in the early phase of your small business's life. Later, more strategic options will be effective in addition to word-of-mouth, your operation's most valuable marketing asset.

5. **Lack of market research.** Why set up a new small business if there are already dozens of other similar operations in your area that have been going successfully for years. If you have a small business idea of merit, ask people you meet and know about the product or service on offer. Just make sure that they're in your target market!

It's always fascinating to hear feedback - and you can adjust your small business marketing plans accordingly. Research costs almost nothing but your time. A bankrupt small business costs much, much more. Research, research, research!

6. **Persisting with a formula that isn't working for too long.** Despite the fact that persistence is vital to small business success, it can be similarly important to know when something *isn't* working and isn't *going to* work.

This is one of the most painful and difficult lessons to learn in small business.

No matter how much we may believe in the idea/product/ service, if the evidence is to the contrary, then it probably isn't going to work in its current form. In such cases, give it a short, finite period, then move on. Persisting with failing advertising is one such act of financial suicide. Many years ago, I started an English tuition small business, Oxford Home Tuition, in Sydney and found that a $50, two-week, fine-tuned classified ad in a select group of local community newspapers at the beginning of the school year delivered more work for that entire year than could possibly be fulfilled - all at $50 an hour!

With advertising and marketing materials, constant experimentation, fine-tuning and monitoring is essential. Similarly, avoid expensive advertising like perceived competitors – they may be clueless too - and try to have your ad situated on the right-hand side of magazines or local newspapers. Left-hand placement response is *much* lower.

Success is what you should be attached to, not a particular idea. When you move on though, try to understand *why* it didn't work and add this to your own knowledge base. Many successful entrepreneurs endured failures before eventually learning how to succeed. We can all learn from that.

7. **Lack of financial resources** *for the project at hand.* There is a world of difference between not having enough money to start *a* small business and not having enough money to start a *particular* small business. As this book will demonstrate, many small businesses can be started with virtually no money and even as an operation parallel to a regular job while it's getting going.

However, trying to start up certain types of small business without enough capital is a certain recipe for failure. This is especially true of small businesses that charge on an account basis and will not see any cash flow from clients for at least 30 days (more like 60-120 days in many cases, if ever).

If a business has salaries, rent and utilities to pay in the interim, there had better be *plenty* in the bank or a *huge* overdraft on hand (which adds interest costs to the business).

8. **'Head in the sand' principle.** Being in business - being alive even - means hearing bad news. Often. Something, somewhere, somebody always screws up and it's going to cost you financially. How should these problems always be dealt with? *Head on.* Talk to creditors. Talk to clients. Talk to

suppliers. Talk to staff - especially about ideas to reduce overheads and increase sales. Keep all problems acknowledged and understood. Denying problems and running away gives *them* the power. Take back that power for yourself. Ultimately, no problem in the world is worth more than your dignity, enjoyment of life and relationships, so treat them accordingly.

9. Crunch the numbers on *everything*. It's like the old expression: count the cents and the dollars will look after themselves. If you need a car for business, does it have to be a new one? Three-year-old cars that are barely run in are usually close to half the price of the new models! Anti-investments (cars, computers, office equipment, furniture) should have a minimum of expenditure whereas investments (shares, property) should have the opposite.

Funny how most of us ignore this basic financial principle and are continually broke. Good tax advice is also critical here.

Where possible, always try to run your small business/es from home - it saves a *fortune*. If you think that $300 per week office rent sounds reasonable, that's $15,000 a year that the owner of that office will get *before* you. And precisely how much bottom-line business will it actually add?

Try to factor all expenses over a monthly and yearly cycle - it gives them a much more realistic perspective.

When dealing with advertising representatives from media publications, be *extremely* firm, stick to an agreed budget before hand and become a black belt at saying 'no'. Insist on *never* paying the full advertising rate – it's an excellent starting point to begin negotiations. Variations in advertising rates are staggering and good hagglers constantly save thousands.

10. Giving up. Don't give up. If you're not succeeding, there are probably sound commercial reasons for it. It has nothing to do with you as a person. Your commercial 'pitch' just needs to change. Talk to a mentor. Talk to people in the business.

Talk to your accountant. Quitting usually means becoming a 'slave monkey' in somebody else's circus. Try, *re-calibrate with external input* and then try again. The only thing that should stop us from continually trying is a pine box. Goethe, the famous German writer and philosopher, who many incredibly smart people regarded as *the* smartest man who ever lived, believed that in life, only one thing mattered: striving.

~

~

2.
*The Perfect
Small Business
Model.*

~

S o, let's summarize. Among the best attributes for small businesses that are successful - not that many businesses have or necessarily need *all* of them - are that:

1. The business can be operated from home (i.e. no giant additional rental overheads).

2. The business does not require a large inventory of product (another financially crippling overhead).

3. The business has several income streams (e.g. service as well as sales - this is how car dealers survive).

4. The business involves a product/service that buyers pay for immediately and *not* on a 30-day/60-day/90-day/120-day basis (late payment of accounts has sent countless small *and* large businesses under).

5. The business relates to the owner's *existing* skills/expertise.

6. The business has a considerable/total *cash-in-hand* sales element.

7. The business earns income when the owner is away (e.g. vending machines).

8. The business is not too reliant on finding good staff (finding and keeping quality staff is one of the biggest issues for all small business operators).

9. The business is not based on too small a number of clients (e.g. an advertising agency with only 1 client) - this gives the client the power and not the business!

10. The business appeals to human *needs* that demand constant fulfillment rather than occasional *wants* (the food retail business is far more bankable than many other 'tertiary' service businesses e.g. people *have to* eat but they don't *need* to have their tarot cards read).

11. The small business has a clear point of *differentiation* from possible competitors e.g. it is faster; it is open after hours when others are closed (like the after hours beauty salon on Page 142); it comes to the client's home; it caters to a specialized niche such as the disabled or gay or senior market; it is much simpler than existing competitors; it is in the best possible location; or it is much cheaper than obvious competitors. Without such a characteristic, a small business will probably struggle.

12. The business is one that the owner clearly enjoys or has some natural affinity with e.g. a car enthusiast importing and selling used Jaguars from Britain.

~

~

3.
The eBay
Mini-Merchant
Revolution:
Your First/Next
Small Business?

~

Surprisingly, eBay is now 10 years old and facilitates transactions in excess of $34 billion annually and that figure keeps growing every year. Countless success stories now abound of small entrepreneurs discovering, maximising and now depending on eBay for their primary income.

Here are the startling numbers on eBay at the moment: 3.5 million+ new items are added every day; every second, $1,000 worth of merchandise is sold; eBay has 135 million+ registered users. As you read these statistics, they are probably already out of date and lower than today's figures.

Now, while eBay has its detractors and certain drawbacks, one fact is undisputed: eBay is nothing short of revolutionary for the small business person seeking to trade in niche merchandise with minimal overheads. In effect, eBay has created a global shopping mall that we can all enjoy as both buyer and seller.

Moreover, one of the best features of eBay is the seller feedback so that buyers can instantly assess the quality of past transactions involving a certain merchant and decide whether to proceed (though 'tit-for-tat' negative feedback is an issue that eBay promised it would fix in May 2008 when it stopped allowing Sellers to give negative feedback on Buyers).

If only the 'real world' had such a feature! Naturally, as a merchant on eBay, you should thus seek to provide a *very* high level of service and therefore keep a high quality feedback percentage.

So, what kind of small business is best suited to an eBay 'shop'?

Here are some of the key attributes:

1. The business is based on a product, not a service.

2. The products being sold are individualistic, niche or non-

mainstream in that they are usually not competing directly with major retailers e.g. specialised jewellery, vintage car parts, antiques, artworks, collectibles, memorabilia and so on (check out http://pages.ebay.com/sellercentral/hotitems.pdf for ideas).

3. The type of product being sold is easily conveyed by quality digital photographs. Learning how to take great, high quality, properly indicative digital photographs is essential.

Countless sales have been lost on eBay through poor photos or listings *without* photos. Madness!

4. The products probably relate to the dealer's expertise, experience or passion. If someone doesn't know a thing about golf - why try to sell golf memorabilia on eBay?

Current eBay bestsellers are published online at:

http://pages.eBay.com/sellercentral/hotitems.pdf

and I have listed a brief sample of this report below.

For more information on the specific mechanics of dealing on and with eBay, these pages are an excellent place to start:

http://pages.ebay.com/education/

http://pages.ebay.com/marketplace_research/

http://pages.ebay.com/sellercentral/

If these websites change since the publication of this book, simply do a search on eBay's site or check through their 'Site Map' to find them. It's in eBay's interest to continually attract new merchants with new products.

Furthermore, Entrepreneur.com has an excellent eBay section where you can read individual success stories across a range of different products (if they did it, so can you, especially with a different product) and get a great deal of useful advice. Check out:

www.entrepreneur.com/ebay/index.html

Similarly, many excellent books are now available (through Amazon.com et al) on running a successful eBay small business. Perhaps the best thing about an online marketplace like eBay is that anyone can monitor the popularity and pricing of *all* advertised products at any moment in real time, at any time of the day. The popularity – or otherwise – of a certain item and its price will be immediately evident in the number of bids received. This invaluable market research is absolutely free.

However, as a starting point for you to consider whether an eBay small business fits your particular personality – the whole point of this book and all its businesses in fact – here is a brief extract from the hottest items from eBay USA in December 2007 where *28 categories of products* are analyzed. Go to:

http://pages.ebay.com/sellercentral/hotitems.pdf

to view the entire report for eBay dealer small business ideas.

Each of the products on eBay's 'Hot Items' list at the above web address could constitute a small business in its own right or, at the very least, provide successful models of other eBay dealers' practises to learn from and apply with a different product/s. You can even pose as a buyer and e-mail questions to eBay dealers to learn more about their products and where they were sourced.

Many outstanding small businesses have been built on a single product or product type and eBay removes most of the 'real-world' financial overheads that destroy too many small business start-ups.

Plus, if these products are proving popular on eBay, they may do well at market stalls too – though experimentation and refinement with your local market is essential.

Report sample extract:

CATEGORY	ITEMS
Coins	<ul><li>American Buffalo Gold Bullion</li><li>Coins-Ancient Greek</li><li>Coins-Great Britain</li><li>Coins-Hungary</li><li>Coins-Middle East India</li><li>Coins-Puerto Rico</li><li>Coins-Turkey</li><li>Coins-US Barber Halves (1892-1915)</li><li>Coins-US Barber Quarters (1892-1916)</li><li>Coins-US Bust Dimes (1796-1837)</li><li>Coins-US Bust Quarters (1796-1838)</li><li>Coins-US Early Commemorative</li><li>Coins-US Gold Eagle $10</li><li>Coins-US Gold Pioneer Fractional</li><li>Coins-US Proof Sets (1990-98)</li><li>Coins-US Seated Liberty Halves (1839-91)</li><li>Coins-US Shield Nickels (1866-83)</li></ul>

~

~
4.
The Single Best
(Free) Research Tools
On The Planet For
Small Business Research.

~

O ne of the best sources of ideas for new small businesses is your local community newspaper. Usually these have large classified sections where successful small business entrepreneurs are conducting their main form of marketing.

Take a good, long look at the types of businesses advertised, how they are advertised, which ads caught your eye, which ones failed to, which offers were appealing, which weren't and so on.

Many of these businesses will have been operating for *decades* so learn from them and learn how to improve on them or their micro-marketing by adding a twist! Where else can you find a list of functional, *surviving* small businesses? CraigsList.org, Gumtree.com and the good old Yellow Pages are similarly useful.

~

~
5.
*10 Powerful
Ways To
Differentiate
Your
Small Business.*

~

I n creating a successful small business, differentiation from existing business products or services is essential. But how can you add a new twist?

Try some of these proven tactics for that extra competitive edge:

1. _Uniqueness **but with existing demand:_** In the vast tracts of business literature out there, everybody talks about creating a unique or sufficiently different identity/product/ service in order to succeed. That's fine but it's only one-third of the equation.

The other two thirds are: (a) that this unique product or service satisfies an *existing* demand (rather than going down the incredibly expensive road of *creating* that demand); and (b) you have to have the patience to educate your target market about this new product or service. Unique yes BUT for existing demand! In fact, most first-to-market competitors lose out to later competitors e.g. iPod, Dell.

2. _Speed:_ By delivering a product or service *much* faster than any competitor is a pretty good recipe for small business success - depending on three critical conditions: (1) your small business can actually *fulfil* that express expectation; (2) the time difference between you and your competitors is quite significant e.g. a pizza delivery store offering 28 minute delivery is unlikely to take away much business from a 30 minute delivery operation; and, (3) the time guarantee becomes synonymous with your business; ideally it even forms part of the business name.

3. _Price:_ Price is obviously a proven winner in attracting and keeping business. If you're using this as your primary marketing advantage, keep in mind that the fulfilment of purchases must still be easy, straightforward and professional plus that the price saving is *perceived* as significant. Perception is everything. Saving $100 on a car purchase will not be perceived as much but $50 on a Blu-Ray DVD player could be. Think of all the price-as-main-marketing-focus types of businesses (they often have the word 'discount' or 'cheap' in the business name) out there.

4. ***Plug the gap:*** This is one of the hardest ways of differentiating the product but is still arguably the best. In short, it involves finding a gap wherein a product or service should be but isn't. What form might this take? Here are some examples: a busy area without a laundromat, writers' reference books without one for unpublished writing contests (one of TheWorldsBiggestBooks.com's most successful past titles, relaunching shortly), a suburb without: a video library, tennis court, newsstand or 7-11. And so on. Train your mind to 'look for the gaps' and they will appear.

That is precisely what the innovative products and services listed in the *X-Files* section of this book starting on Page 89 attempt to do.

Don't ever have the pessimistic belief that every single thing has *already* been covered. Major new ideas come along all the time, hundreds of which are listed in this book, that totally disprove this defeatist myth e.g. the internet, fax machines, cellphones, credit cards, cable TV (remember when there were none of these?).

5. ***Convenience:*** This could be tied into location or speed but basically you make the process of doing something much more convenient. For example, you bring a service to the client's home rather than having them come to a central location. Some mortgage services do this. Many don't. For busy workers, the home consultation or, better still, online application, is far more convenient. Like paying bills over the internet or via phone or having dry cleaning picked up from your home. Think of the tasks or errands that you need to take care of in your own life and how a savvy small business might make that job more convenient. That's one way that great new small business ideas start.

6. ***Added value:*** Given that perception is *everything* in marketing (just ask BMW!), adding *perceived* value to a

purchase is a proven method of differentiating products and services. The new car business is a typical example with longer warranties, free air-conditioning, free-servicing and 0% finance all on offer now as brands try to set themselves apart from each other.

The real trick with adding value is that the additional items must *not* cost the business a great deal more in raw materials or time but must have a reasonably high *perceived* value.

Simple examples in businesses today include offers like: free Coke with any burger purchased, music CDs/DVD movies with Sunday newspapers, one month free with a 12 month ISP contract (actually *only* an 8% discount when calculated!), frequent flyer miles, 1 week/month free rent on a 12 month lease etc. Adding value can push potential buyers across the threshold (raise the 'buying temperature') into becoming actual customers - something that all good businesses do every day (often *solely* through the quality of staff interactions with the target market). *The conversion of prospects into customers is one of your primary goals.*

7. **Location:** For entrepreneurs in the real world and through online 'real estate' (e.g. Amazon for small publishers), the location of your business will be critical to its success. In short, 'go fishing where the fish are'. But there's more to the location factor than first meets the eye. For example, it may be of more benefit to be in a more competitive area with a larger target market than a smaller one with few competitors. It may also be that a certain town or community is missing a number of potential businesses - this is particularly so in the current age with the gradual drift of people to larger cities. Agencies that represent *several* services are one opportunity in such communities. Or, it may be that your small business *needs* to be on a busy road. In retail, this can obviously have a huge bearing on success.

8. **The Deal:** Simply by changing the structure of something - the sale or deal - can have enormous consumer appeal. Examples of this from the 'real world' include buyback schemes

after 2 years for new cars at an agreed 50% of the new price, 1 year interest free loans on furniture and electrical, leasing a car through a 'novated' agreement involving an employer and employee, free DVD player in return for one year's DVD rentals, no deposit home loans, 'no docs' home loans and so on.

In each instance, the deal was restructured to make it *seem* far more attractive or to take out an element of *perceived* difficulty. In reality, each of the businesses still got what they were after - a sale! All they did was change one aspect of 'the deal' - a mental hurdle for the buyer was thus removed.

Upon close inspection, very little was sacrificed in the way of profit to make the deal far more attractive. Even the 'no deposit' home loan involved a higher rate of interest *and* making the loan applicant use that home construction company - these would easily compensate the company for any 'loss' up front.

9. ***Quality:*** Generally speaking, small businesses are operated fairly poorly across the world. It seems that many small business operators have low expectations of themselves, their business and even their clients. This attitude can take many forms: poor business presentation, lack of punctuality, focus on problems rather than capabilities, antagonism towards customers and so on.

However, those small business operators that clearly *do care* about their business earn tremendous REPEAT business and repeat business is *the* cornerstone of small business success.

For example, my mechanic is so friendly, fast, flexible and professional that I wouldn't dream of *ever* taking my car anywhere else again - even after I moved to the other side of the city and it was inconvenient to get to him! Over my lifetime, I will spend thousands and thousands of dollars with him and feel very happy about it. Similarly, I often drive past a local pie shop on a busy road that has a long queue that reaches *outside* the shop *every* lunch hour - queues outside a pie shop? Who's ever seen or heard of such a thing?

A great product isn't just the actual product though - everything about a business from the cleanliness of the store to the quality of phone communication is a part of the experience of doing business. In a way, because it is done so poorly so much, it makes the good ones stand out even more and customers cling to them with tenacious loyalty! That's what you want from your customers and clients - tenacious loyalty, great (free) word-of-mouth advertising and *repeat business.*

That's the best kind of 'loyalty program' imaginable - great service for happy *repeat* buyers.

10. ***Communication:*** Like the issue of quality above, the power and style with which your business communicates internally *and* externally is critical to your business success. You *and* your staff should always answer inquiries with professionalism, helpfulness and 'non-pushy' enthusiasm.

Ever been into a store where the staff are talking to each other about their party last night or ex-boyfriend's annoying habits? Such discussions tell customers that this business is poorly run and that management doesn't give a damn about the shoppers' experience. Every detail about a business communicates a message to the world: is the store clean? Are the staff well dressed and groomed? How do staff members talk to each other (I've lost count of the number of times staff have abused each other in front of me and other customers - stores I've never returned to!)? Are staff members polite on the phone? Do the staff know what they are talking about? Will the staff help a shopper with large items to their car and do it happily?

Disappointed customers often don't complain - they just never, ever return.

Among the numerous details of running a business, these 'transactional moments' all leave *impressions* on customers and influence their decision whether to use your business again or to recommend your business to a friend. Seems important now doesn't it?

But all of the above requires *leadership*! The culture of a business is a reflection of the inner world of its leader/s. The buck starts and stops with the leader!

Incidentally, most people assume that leadership is about leading *others*. In fact, a good or great leader leads *themselves* firstly in terms of discipline, values, hard work, social skills, and knowledge/skill acquisition. Others then naturally *follow* such a leader.

An implied goal therefore is for the business owner - like you! - to strive to become a 'black belt' in terms of leadership of themselves. Any individual who masters this aspect of their life cannot help but be extremely successful.

Of course, the primary business goal is to convert *potential* buyers into *actual* buyers. The higher the conversion rate, the more money can be made and the more that expansion is possible.

In so doing, these factors - especially leadership - will influence The Conversion Rate. It's everything in business.

And, as with most things in life, the fundamental question is this:

How would I like to be treated if the roles were reversed?

A part of any small business communication strategy will, of course, be its marketing and vehicles like CraigsList.org, Gumtree.com, local community newspapers offer excellent bang-for-your-buck.

~

~

6.

*10 Ways To Save
Thousands of Dollars
In Your Small Business.*

~

H ere are several ways to save thousands and thousands of dollars for your business over the course of its life:

1. *Work from home.* Obviously cutting out the expense of renting office or professional space somewhere means that (much more) money stays in *your* pocket. Try hard to make this principle work for you - it could be the difference between success and failure. Remember, the landlord gets paid *before* you and your family.

2. *Shop around on everything.* It's a proven yet surprising fact that people will haggle more over a used car than a massive mortgage. Putting aside the bewildering reasons for this, the point is to *always* shop around on significant purchases - ask yourself if you *need* the 'thing' to be new or whether a 'youngish' used item will suffice in the short to medium term. All those savings add up to dollars in *your* pocket. It's hard enough making money these days - remember that most small businesses make around 20% net profit - without throwing it away on extravagant new stuff that will be a boring debt burden in a week or less. In a way, winning the small business 'game', or even in life generally, is as much about 'reprogramming' yourself as all of the other aspects of the venture.

Shop around on phone company rates, cell phone deals, stationery, office equipment including computers, furniture - everything! Three year-old cars cost less than half of new cars yet still feel pretty new to drive. After your business has 93 branches in 16 countries, that's the time to buy wasteful new stuff like a groovy MacBook Air.

3. *Needs not wants.* When you are shopping around for stuff for your business as per the above point, you have to be clear on whether your business really needs this 'thing' or if it is just an impulsive whim. I'm always staggered in big office supplies stores by the small business people there who seem like kids buying toys - they love getting new gadgets. But does their business really need it? The guiding principle is to spend with the head (rational) not the heart (emotional) - think of it as good practice for the rest of your business.

4. *Thoroughly research tax-deductibility.* Before you spend a dime! Think of the feeling of discovering a year or two down the track in your small business that you could have saved thousands of dollars through tax deductibility. *Saving money is equivalent to earning money.* Except that it's actually easier.

The real trick in small business is to save money in ways that customers and clients *don't see*. To them, your operation should appear immaculately professional and thorough.

5. *Exhaust low-cost and no-cost marketing* before the more expensive forms of marketing. A good place to begin is the chapter in this book entitled: *25 Great Places To Freely/Cheaply Advertise Your Small Business* on Page 83. In advertising, I always found that a good classified ad would deliver far more business than a giant display ad. Why? Mainly because the classified ad *targeted* the market with real precision and did half the qualifying for us. If someone is looking for an exhaust pipe for a 1975 Mustang, they go straight to the relevant classified section or on eBay. Plus, research shows that we readers are increasingly 'tuning out' to big display ads (even though they cost an absolute fortune!).

Think small but targeted! Precision marketing *not* blanket coverage. To demonstrate the importance of this approach, calculate how many clients/customers your small business will need. You might find that it is surprisingly low. A home tuition business should only need 20-25 clients to generate returns of $1,200-$1,500 a week! So now, out of the tens of thousands of readers of that local paper, such a business only needs to reach 20-25 clients! The cost of placing that classified is obviously quite low compared to those sorts of returns.

6. *Practicality not prestige.* One of the characteristics of the age we live in is the voracious desire for prestige. While this could be a useful basis for some form of small business, it should *not* guide the policies, decision-making or day-to-day operations of a business (unless related to necessary company image e.g. a premier valet service like the Brit who charges celebrities $10,000 for a car wash on Page 90!).

This isn't exactly rocket science but many small business newbies fail to assess *all* decisions on the basis of business practicality, not prestige. A good guide is to ask yourself when making purchases or decisions: *am I doing this out of strength or out of weakness?* Is a Mercedes really four times better than a Toyota? No way. When your business *is* successful, *then* you can enjoy the fruits of that labor but to do so too early could be disastrous.

7. *Use the internet.* One of the great things about the age we live in is access to information and the interactivity provided by the internet. Knowing how to research online skilfully (obviously through the ubiquitous Google, clusty.com and www.Ask.com) will enrich your small business knowledge considerably and your small business could, and probably should, have an online presence - consumers rightly expect it now. If you do have an online presence, make sure it's as well attended as the rest of the business. One service that will help in this respect is www.humanclick.com that allows you/your staff to be like shop assistants online.

8. *Software angles.* Software for business costs a huge amount of money. Some versions of Microsoft Office cost over US$500! There are alternatives though. Did you know, for example, that Google offer a free online word processor (http://docs.google.com) that is fully compatible with Microsoft Word? As long as you are online, you can write, save and access all the word processing power you are ever likely to need. Plus, if you are enrolled in a part-time study course at a tertiary institution, you can access the same software in 'Academic Versions' - highly reduced in price (in some cases, less than 25% of full price). www.openoffice.org is also worth a look for free office software.

Or, if you don't share files externally, take a look at StarOffice (http://www.sun.com/software/star/staroffice/index.jsp) - a complete Office suite for about US$70. These do much the same as Microsoft's Office but without the eye-popping price.

9. ***Choose the right business structure.*** Depending on the type of business you wish to operate, choosing the right business structure is imperative. Why? Because each type of structure - depending on laws in your area - will have very different tax and legal implications. Selecting the wrong one could cause major problems (read 'expense') further down the track. To work out the right structure, consult with an accountant (or two!) indicating the type of business and rough annual turnover of your business. She or he can then guide you on which path to take.

10. ***Use the 'just in time' principle.*** Large-scale manufacturers apply this principle to avoid having money tied up in inventory. This principle means that items necessary for the business or product are purchased *just* before their use. In short, the operation using this approach does not have six months worth of advance supplies sitting in a warehouse or garage. That's money that has been spent that isn't working for your business that could be used elsewhere e.g. marketing. The one possible exception to this rule could be where an *extraordinary* deal is on offer and to miss the opportunity would mean losing an opportunity to maximise a higher profit. The one caveat here is that you must be certain that the stock will sell. *If there is doubt, then there is no doubt - don't do it.*

Think of money as a tool or weapon - personally I quite like Suze Orman's slightly New Age concept that money should be conceived as a kind of energy and if we are putting out great energy into the world, then that will naturally attract money.

~

~
7.
The
Best Quotes
Of All Time
About Business.

~

~

"It's not *what* you sell that matters.
It's *how* you sell it."
Anon

'The success of every single business in the world hinges on
how well it *communicates* - with clients, potential clients,
suppliers, stakeholders, within itself and with the world.'
John Norrie

'No one will ever need more than 637Kb of memory
for a personal computer.'
Bill Gates

'You can never quit.
Winners never quit and quitters never win.'
Ted Turner

'Management is nothing more than
motivating other people.'
Lee Iacocca

'A pessimist sees the difficulty in every opportunity,
an optimist sees the opportunity in every difficulty.'
Winston Churchill

'Destiny is not a matter of chance;
it is a matter of choice.'
William Jennings Bryan

'Eighty percent of success is just showing up.'
Woody Allen

'Everybody lives by selling something.'
Robert Louis Stevenson

~

~

'If opportunity doesn't knock, build a door.'
Milton Berle

'Give me a stock clerk with a goal, and I will
give you a man who will make history.
Give me a man without a goal
and I will give you a stock clerk.'
J. C. Penney

'If you can dream it, you can do it.'
Walt Disney

'Imagination is more important than knowledge.'
Albert Einstein

'None are so old as those who have
outlived their enthusiasm.'
Henry David Thoreau

'Nothing in the world can take the place of persistence.'
Calvin Coolidge

'Nothing is more difficult, and therefore more precious,
than to be able to decide.'
Napoleon

'The people who own small businesses
in this country work far more than
they should for the return they're getting.'
Michael E. Gerber

'The real secret of success is enthusiasm.'
Walter Chrysler

~

~

'Thinking is the hardest work there is,
which is why so few people engage in it.'
Henry Ford

'We have met the enemy, and it is us.'
Walt Kelly

'What would you attempt to do if
you knew you could not fail?'
Robert Schuller

'Whether you think you can,
or think you can't, you're right.'
Henry Ford

'To carry on a successful business,
a man must have imagination.'
Charles M Schwab

'Nothing focuses the mind better than the constant sight of a
competitor who wants to wipe you off the map.'
Wayne Calloway

'Our favourite (stock) holding period is forever.'
Warren Buffet

'If everyone is thinking alike,
then somebody isn't thinking.'
General Patton

~

~

'The whole purpose of a business is
to create and *keep* customers.'
Theodore Levitt

'An objective of leadership is to help
those who are doing poorly to do well
and to help those who are doing well to do even better.'
Jim Rohn

'Management works *in* the system.
Leadership works *on* the system.'
Stephen R. Covey

'Outstanding leaders go out of the way to boost the self-esteem
of their personnel. If people believe in themselves,
it's amazing what they can accomplish.'
Sam Walton

Man is not a rational animal, he is a rationalizing animal.
Robert A. Heinlein

'Treat people with a recognition of their potential,
not their current state of development.'
Teaching axiom

'Striving is everything.'
Goethe

'Business is about converting prospects into customers.
Everything else is secondary.'
John Norrie

~

~
8.
*The Top New
Product/Service Ideas
in History.*

~

I t's funny how new ideas or inventions seem so simple and obvious when they're released - take the new products in the *X-Files* section of this book on Page 89 for example. The rest of the world seems to say: 'why didn't I think of that?' Well, one of the obvious reasons is that 'they' weren't *trying* to think of a new product or service. In reality, can any entrepreneur come up with a hot new concept if they aren't in the *mental habit* of thinking, creating and problem solving?

This latter point cannot be underestimated. However, the reality is that great new ideas are actually pretty common in today's world. As TV programs like *Dragons' Den* illustrate, the key difference between a great idea and a killer small business is *action*. The 'Big Idea' *must* be fully followed through on with action in order to realise its potential. The solution to an existing *problem* is the impulse behind many of these extraordinary ideas below.

One other principle that cannot be underestimated is that many of the ideas or products below that have proven incredibly successful were never originally conceived for the purpose they were eventually popular in - the internet and fax machine are two such examples. The internet, for example, was only ever intended as a means for university researchers to share information.

While we may take many of these below ideas for granted now, there was a time when they did not exist - it took someone to have the *original* idea or *application* of that idea and then to fully *act* on that idea:

Internet	Fire
McDonald's/The Franchise	Wheel
Facebook	Combustion Engine
MySpace	Yo-yo
eBay	Automobile
Google	Airplane
Razor Scooter	Bicycle
Coca-Cola	Jeans
Compact Disc/DVD	Electricity

And what about these?

Battery	Microwave oven
Fax machine	Penicillin
Lego	Pencil
Barbie Doll	Printing press/books
Light bulb	Refrigerator
Zipper	Rubik's cube
Phone/cellphone	Radio
Television	Typewriter
Air conditioner	Hovercraft
Automobile	Liquid paper
Dynamite	Computer modem
Laser	Camera
Super glue	Watch/clock
VCR	Answering machine
Infomercials	Bubble wrap
Home Delivered Pizza	Democracy
Black box flight recorder	Ice
Non-stick frying pan	Wrench
Audio cassette	Nails/screws
Biro	*Big Brother*
Space-bags	Propeller
Kitty litter	Dry cleaning
Calculator	Drive-thru fast-food
Computer mouse	Postage stamps
Bar-codes	Credit cards
Floppy disk	Scales
Blender	Stapler
Bottled water	Elevator/escalator
Video libraries	Insurance
Balloons	RFID tags
Sewing machine	Bean bag
Paint	Plastic bag
Traffic lights	Lay-away/lay-by
Flip-flops	Body piercing

~

Maslow's Hierarchy of (Human) Needs

This valuable psychological tool - check out a full explanation at http://en.wikipedia.org/wiki/Maslow's_hierarchy_of_needs - indicates the hierarchy of importance for humans in the prioritization of their activities:

TOP
Self-Actualization
Realization of individual potential.

Esteem Needs
Self-esteem, respect of others.

Love Needs
Love, belonging, family, affirmation, friendship, bonding.

Safety Needs
Security of shelter, home, safety.

BOTTOM
Physiological Needs
Hunger, thirst, sex, sleep, air.

Which need will your small business appeal to? Typically, the safer forms of business occupy the lower rungs of this table. Individuals with more money ascend while those without it tend to remain at or near the bottom.

~

~
9.
To Buy
Into A Franchise
Or Not?
~

F ranchising is obviously a massive industry and constitutes one of the main pathways into small business for those seeking to master their own professional destiny.

Yes, franchises generally have a lower failure rate than 'normal' small businesses. However, before rushing into considerable debt and a long-term contractual relationship with a franchising corporation, there are at least THREE serious questions you must ask:

1. Does the franchise in question actually have any *brand equity* i.e. is the franchise brand name known in the community and is it known for the right reasons? Ask people around you who would use such a service. If nobody has ever heard of the franchise, why pay franchising fees when you could simply establish a (better/cheaper/faster) 'copycat' rival business where you keep 100% of the profits for as long as the business keeps going - at which point, you could sell it, of course. Beware hyperbolic profit and sales projections from franchising companies. Did you know that major class actions from disgruntled franchisees over the exaggeration of expected returns are now underway in the US? *Buyer beware,* of course, as in all things, but *especially* with a franchise.

2. Have you approached several 'real world' franchise holders of the brand you are thinking about, paid them for their time - an hour should do it - and asked them for an independent, practical-not-theoretical and 'warts-and-all' assessment of the value of the franchise? It could be the best investment you have ever made and you should do this by simply walking in, introducing yourself and asking for an hour of the franchisee's time for which you will pay an agreed price over a nice meal which you will pay for. This step seems absolutely critical and obvious yet it is one that many new franchisees never do. Incredible!

These existing small business operators could save your financial future and paint a picture *vastly* different from the company seeking to attract new franchisees. Even if the purchase of the franchise goes ahead, the advice from these individuals is incredibly valuable as they can advise you against costly errors that *they* made and wish they had avoided.

If you proceed with the franchise purchase, they may even turn out to be a good mentor/friend for you in the future if you hit it off.

The flaw in human nature that some franchise companies are working with here in the aspiring small business entrepreneur's is that *they want to believe* that the massive sales and profit projections are true - just like a new 'wonder' diet pill or 'revolutionary' new exercise machine. *Wanting* to believe that something is true obviously has little bearing on reality.

3. Does the main action of the business suit your personality well or is it merely a money-making exercise? It will prove much harder to succeed if the day-to-day *action* of the small business franchise does not suit your personality.

One final thought: it is a statistical fact that franchises have a much higher success rate than 'normal' small business start ups. Michael E. Gerber explores this phenomenon in the must-read, *The E-myth: Why Most Businesses Don't Work and What to Do About It.*

The point is to analyse and *deconstruct* exactly *why* franchises succeed and apply those principles to your own start-up.

~

~

10.
Is
'Owning Your Own Job'
So Bad?

~

One aspect of small business advice in print and person that has always troubled me is the often-repeated view that there is no point in 'owning a job' when it comes to small business. This term is taken to mean that there is no point in giving up a 'regular job' where you work for someone else just to be self-employed. The accepted wisdom goes that unless you can establish a business that does *not* require your presence to function, then that business venture is a waste of time.

Here are three reasons why I profoundly disagree:

1. Small business is about finding a means of supporting oneself financially in a way *compatible* with that person's particular *personality*. Many individuals simply prefer to be their own boss and aren't suited to life in a large firm or working for others. In this sense, having a small business as a self-employed person can be a brilliant way to enhance individual happiness - even if the business does not function or earn income while the owner is absent and even if the income earned is about the same as being a 'normal' employee.

In fact, such individuals feel empowered and quite contented earning their *own* income on *their* terms and thus 'owning a job' is clearly a pathway to personal happiness. What could be more important than that? Building a massive franchised empire is not every person's aspiration and simply having control over one's professional income is all that is needed and desired as other priorities such as family, hobbies, interests and a more relaxed lifestyle also constitute aspects of a happy, meaningful life.

2. The simple fact is that very few individuals can quit their regular job on a Friday and own a fully-functioning, profitable small business on the following Monday. Self-employment where an individual 'owns a job' is thus a fantastic 'stepping stone' from one mode of economic survival to another. After establishing oneself in self-employment, being the boss, making all the decisions and learning the art of small business, an eventual step into a self-sustaining business is thus much

simpler and much more likely to succeed.

3. In the early phase of many small businesses, the naïve approach of the business owners is such that crippling overhead expenses in the form of leases, staffing and other equipment mean that there is very little, if any, profit. Ironically, the individual owning their own business in the form of self-employment – especially in a knowledge-based or service-based industry - often earns a great deal *more* profit simply by only employing themselves.

Besides personal happiness, profit is the ultimate goal, not the egotism of trying to build a flashy, obvious empire quickly and this sense, many self-employed 'sole traders' leave other small businesses for dead.

~

~

11.
25 Great Places To
Freely/Cheaply
Advertise Your
Small Business.

~

I n advertising and marketing your shiny new small business, it is essential to build from a very, very low cost base - unless you are related to someone with shares in the oil business. Have you considered these fantastic options below for no-cost or very low cost advertising for your small business? Remember, decades of real-world advertising experience says that a well-written, well-targeted classified ad far outperforms a giant, colourful full page spread. It's counter-intuitive but to succeed in any business, being able to embrace the 'counter-intuitive' is a critical mental ability. Most people can't and thus fail.

CraigsList.org/Gumtree.com/Backpage.com
(Free community online advertising mediums)

Local paper classifieds
(*Not* the city-wide majors like *The New York Times*)

A4 horizontal flyers on bright paper placed on noticeboards in relevant sites
(e.g. college coffee shops, if relevant for your targets)

DM letterbox drops
(Created in Microsoft Word & printed on brightly-colored paper from your PC, hand delivered by you/your children to your entire neighbourhood)

Per-click Web advertising through Google
(On specific keywords and phrases e.g. "Denver lapidary classes" but monitor this channel closely as costs can *quickly* escalate; general terms like "used cars" are normally way too expensive to consider)

Blogs that focus on your small business area
(e.g. "Gold Prospecting", start at www.blogger.com)

Yahoo! Groups in your specific area
(These are free discussion forums where you can discuss your thoughts and expertise but don't self-promote too blatantly, start at http://groups.yahoo.com)

Advertising on relevant newsletters/e-zines
(E-zines/newsletters are electronic magazines,
a very fast way of reaching your target market.
Search at clusty.com for ones in your small business area)

Yellow Pages
(Ensure that the 'Online Advertising' option is also selected)

On Your Vehicle
(With a magnetic sign that can be removed when 'off-duty'
e.g. www.magneticsignsontime.com;
www.custom-magnets.com/car_door_magnets.htm;
www.ocsigns.com/magneticpricing.htm)

Your own small business website
(Brilliant web template ideas at:
www.templatemonster.com
www.hypertemplates.com)

Submit articles on your small business area to:
http://ezinearticles.com
http://goarticles.com
(When others read them, they could/should be motivated to
visit your site)

Answer reader queries in your small business area on:
http://answers.yahoo.com

Wikipedia
(Get your business listed as a Wikipedia entry so that
search engines will pick up your home page)

Banner Advertising on Sites That Your Targets Visit
(e.g. If you are targeting amateur writers, get banner
advertising on Moira Allen's brilliant
www.writing-world.com)

Yahoo! Business Express Site Submission
(Yes they are asking an outrageous $299 for "consideration"
but it's worth it for a decent listing on Yahoo!
Start at https://ecom.yahoo.com/dir/submit/intro)

Submit your small business website (often)
to these locations:
www.dmoz.org/add.html
www.superpages.com
(Go to "Add or Edit a Business")
www.google.com/addurl/

Post classifieds and blogs on:
MySpace.com

Grocery docket ads/Grocery store noticeboard
(In some territories, ad space can be purchased on the back of
grocery dockets. Look also at a posting on the grocery store
noticeboard, they're usually free and your small business
should have a posting in every supermarket in your
catchment area.)

Media Interviews
(If your small business has an interesting new angle - it better!
- then approach local community radio stations and
newspapers with a press release.
These sites have excellent press release writing advice:
www.lunareclipse.net/pressrelease.htm
www.publicityinsider.com/release.asp
www.netpress.org/careandfeeding.html)

Word-Of-Mouth
(Actually *ask* your best customers to recommend you
to their friends)

Business Cards
(Make sure that you have very professional business cards to
give to people you randomly meet)

~

~

12.
The X-Files:
The Latest & Greatest
Unusual, Strange & Intriguing
New Small Business
Ideas.

~

★ *Sugar Jewellery (i.e. jewellery made of sugar)*
CONCEPT: Kids will love this: edible jewellery! It looks like jewellery but can be eaten like candy when the wearer gets bored with it.
COMPANY/INVENTOR: Greetje van Helmond
FURTHER INFO: www.greetjevanhelmond.com

★ *Air-Powered Car*
CONCEPT: The *Aircar* is a 350kg fibreglass car that runs on compressed air that can be refilled in three minutes and has no emissions – expected sale price is around $5,000.
COMPANY/INVENTOR: Tata/Guy Negre/Moteur Development International
FURTHER INFO: http://business.timesonline.co.uk/tol/business/industry_sectors/transport/article3399532.ece; http://news.bbc.co.uk/1/hi/sci/tech/7241909.stm

★ *'Shark Shield' Shark Deterrent*
CONCEPT: The alliteratively-entitled *Shark Shield* gives sharks of all types the cold shoulder by "an electric field that induces spasms in the sharks' snouts." Ouch. It thus enhances safety for divers, surfers, swimmers and shark wrestlers. Apparently, it is physically harmless to the sharks but does bruise their ego.
COMPANY/INVENTOR: SA Govt
FURTHER INFO: www.sharkshield.com

★ *Cheeseburger In A Can*
CONCEPT: As an alternate food source for camping and travelling in the wild, the 'Canned Cheeseburger' is an interesting way to capitalise on a fast food staple of Western civilisation.
COMPANY/INVENTOR: Katadyn/Trekking-Mahlzeiten
FURTHER INFO: www.trekking-mahlzeiten.de

★ *Waterless Urinal*
CONCEPT: *ZeroFlush* is a waterless urinal that – according to the manufacturer – can save over 150,000 litres of fresh water per year/per urinal. In a world running short of resources like water, products like this one have an obvious market.
COMPANY/INVENTOR: Brightwater (Caroma have a similar product now too, the *H2Zero Cube Urinal*)
FURTHER INFO: www.bwater.eu/zeroflush/

★ *The Tweel Rubberless Wheel*
CONCEPT: Michelin have developed an "airless, integrated tyre and wheel" (think a wheel *without* a tire, like a kind of small metal wagon wheel) that creates wheels far more durable than ever before and can be fitted to wheelchairs, Segues and eventually passenger cars. The *Tweel* removes many of the problems associated with conventional pneumatic tyres.
COMPANY/INVENTOR: Michelin
FURTHER INFO: Search on a Michelin site in your territory with the keyword, "Tweel".

★ *'Affordable' Recreational Submarine*
CONCEPT: A Dutch company now offers recreational submarines that have a top speed of 3.5 mph, can submerge to 50 metres and weigh around a ton – pricing is approximately $130,000 per submarine.
COMPANY/INVENTOR: Uboatworx
FURTHER INFO: www.uboatworx.com

★ *$10,000/£5,000 Car Wash For Celebrities*
CONCEPT: By offering a week-long, 61-step car wash with rare Brazilian wax called Zymol Royale wax, witty Brit Paul Dalton has built a fiercely loyal celebrity following in Britain who are happy to have their exotic cars lovingly TLCed by him. For $10,000 per car wash.

And he is about to put his prices up.
COMPANY/INVENTOR: Pinnacle Wash
FURTHER INFO: www.edmunds.com/insideline/do/News/articleId=114981

★ *Mail-To-Images Scanning & Recycling Service*
CONCEPT: One way to recycle is to have somebody else do it for you. For example, Earth Class Mail can scan your mail and securely e-mail it to you as images and recycle the paper. Apparently very little mail waste is presently recycled.
COMPANY/INVENTOR: Earth Class Mail Corp
FURTHER INFO: www.earthclassmail.com

★ *Water Purifying Drinking Straw*
CONCEPT: Intended for use in countries where water quality is suspect, the *Lifestraw* can prevent exposure to Shigella, Salmonella, Staphylococcus Aureus and E .Coli.
COMPANY/INVENTOR: Vestergaard Frandsen
FURTHER INFO: www.waterstraws.com

★ *'Snowter' BMX Ski Bike*
CONCEPT: The *Snowter* is an Austrian cross between a snowboard and a BMX bike and as the photos on the company website prove, it looks pretty stoopid but then so did the *Hoola Hoop* when it first came out.
COMPANY/INVENTOR: XOIOX/Martin Trebichavsky KEG
FURTHER INFO: www.snowter.com

★ *Switchboard Snowboard*
CONCEPT: The *Switchboard* is basically a snowboard with mountain bike handles that offers more stunt possibilities than a conventional snowboard.
COMPANY/INVENTOR: Venom Switchboards
FURTHER INFO: www.venomsnow.com

★ *Portable Espresso Maker*
CONCEPT: From the ever-expanding world of high-tech camping equipment comes the *Handpresso Wild*, a lightweight espresso maker that only requires hot water in order to work.
COMPANY/INVENTOR: Handpresso
FURTHER INFO: www.handpresso.fr

★ *Fully Retractable Umbrella*
CONCEPT: The *Lotus 23* is a self-cleaning (think rainy water), fully-retractable umbrella with flexible ribs that allow it to flow with the wind. It is also cheaper to manufacture and more durable than a conventional umbrella.
COMPANY/INVENTOR: Andy Wana
FURTHER INFO: www.joshspear.com/item/lotus-23-reinventing-the-umbrella/

★ *'Living' Triceratops Toy*
CONCEPT: Playskool have released a 40" tall, semi-robotic Triceratops that can move its head, mouth, horns and tail in addition to movement sensors.
COMPANY/INVENTOR: Playskool
FURTHER INFO: www.pr-inside.com/believe-in-play-hasbro-s-playskool-r439591.htm

★ *In-Store Surfing Simulator*
CONCEPT: Originally available on cruise ships and in water theme parks, the *FlowRider* uses pressurized water to create an indoor surfing simulation experience with wakeboards.
COMPANY/INVENTOR: Adrenalina
FURTHER INFO: www.adrenalinastore.com

★ *T-Shirt Air Cannon*
CONCEPT: Created as a sports venue novelty, Air

Cannons can fire t-shirts far into the air and their range (dependent on model) and direction can be controlled. They can also be used to promote businesses and for company promotions.

COMPANY/INVENTOR: Air Cannons Inc
FURTHER INFO: www.aircannonsinc.com

★ *Soccer Ball Vending Machine*
CONCEPT: Nike has developed football vending machines – perfect for special edition balls that are not available in normal retail channels. As Nike stared this program in Singapore in 2005, these machines should be starting to turn up on the second-hand market and thus offer an interesting business proposition.

COMPANY/INVENTOR: Nike
FURTHER INFO: www.mediabuyerplanner.com/
2005/09/19/nike_launches_soccer_ball/

★ *iPod Vending Machine*
CONCEPT: A company specializing in 'automated retailing' now offers iPods through vending machines. They also sell Elizabeth Arden cosmetics, digital cameras and other electronic products via sophisticated vending machines.

COMPANY/INVENTOR: Zoom Systems
FURTHER INFO: www.zoomsystems.com

★ *Free Photocopies on Advertising-Sided Paper*
CONCEPT: Tadacopy in Japan offers students free photocopying though there is no reason why the business model could not work more broadly. The revenue comes from advertising placed on the reverse side of the paper.

COMPANY/INVENTOR: See above
REAL WORLD BIZ: www.tadacopy.com

★ *Hair Straightener Vending Machine*
CONCEPT: One innovative UK company has released a form of vending machine that allows (predominantly women?) users to straighten unruly hair with the device. Perfect for women's bathrooms everywhere.
COMPANY/INVENTOR: Beautiful Vending
FURTHER INFO: www.beautifulvending.com

★ *Acting Troupe for Home Performance Hire*
CONCEPT: *Teatr Rozmaitosci* in Warsaw, Poland, offer clients an in-home theatrical performance from a group of professional actors - what a party or dinner novelty!
COMPANY/INVENTOR: See above
FURTHER INFO: www.springwise.com/ entertainment/teatr_rozmaitosci/

★ *Drink-Mixing Vending Machines*
CONCEPT: In another interesting vending machine variation, a British company has created a machine capable of mixing drinks and requiring far fewer top-ups than conventional machines through an innovative internal pouch system.
COMPANY/INVENTOR: WaterWerkz
FURTHER INFO: www.waterwerkz.co.uk

★ *Ice Cream Vending Machine*
CONCEPT: A clever Massachusetts firm have created an ice cream vending machine capable of offering up to 12 flavours and 6 mix-ins at once. Yum.
COMPANY/INVENTOR: MooBella
FURTHER INFO: www.moobella.com

★ *Recycling Vending Machine*
CONCEPT: Users bring empty beverage containers to this 'reverse vending' unit and the machine sorts the materials into recyclable groups and crushes it. Income is

made by being the local supplier of such machines to governments, schools and large organizations and emptying them.

COMPANY/INVENTOR: Reverse Vending Corporation

FURTHER INFO: www.reversevending.co.uk

★ *90 Second Dual Pizza Oven*

CONCEPT: One of the mantras of successful small business initiatives is to 'do it faster' than your competitors. This 1440-watt high-speed pizza oven certainly fits that criterion.

COMPANY/INVENTOR: Via Hammacher Schlemmer

FURTHER INFO: www.hammacher.com/publish/ 75085.asp

★ *Sun Screen Vending Machine*

CONCEPT: If situated near a popular beach, this automated sunscreen and tanning mist vending machine/booth should do extremely well.

COMPANY/INVENTOR: Sunscreen Mist

FURTHER INFO: www.sunscreenmist.com

★ *Crucifix MP3 Player*

CONCEPT: An MP3/WMA (Windows Media Audio) player in the shape of a cross to appeal to young Christian music fans.

COMPANY/INVENTOR: See websites below

FURTHER INFO: www.chinavasion.com/ product_info.php/pName/cross-mp3-player-1gb-two-color-lcd-display/; www.vavolo.com

★ *Toy Rentals For Kids*

CONCEPT: Parents can rent toys for a set monthly subscription fee (that is much lower than the price of purchasing the toys) and return them when their children

become bored with them.
COMPANY/INVENTOR: Baby Plays
FURTHER INFO: www.babyplays.com

★ *Baby Clothes Rentals*
CONCEPT: One German company offers baby clothes for rent in order that parents don't waste money on children quickly outgrowing their wardrobe.
COMPANY/INVENTOR: Luette Leihen
FURTHER INFO: www.luette-leihen.de (German language website)

★ *Heinz Bean Bars*
CONCEPT: In London, Heinz have created a pub where the baked beans are 'poured' from the taps – there are even different flavours 'on tap'.
COMPANY/INVENTOR: Heinz
FURTHER INFO: www.adcult.com/ads/baked-bean/; http://uk.youtube.com/watch?v=YGTt6kAYCOI

★ *Animated Business Cards*
CONCEPT: Based on 'magic motion' card technology that has been around for some time, these animated business cards definitely leave an impression.
COMPANY/INVENTOR: Chung Dha
FURTHER INFO: http://blog.makezine.com/archive/2008/02/animated_business_card.html?CMP=OTC-0D6B48984890; http://uk.youtube.com/watch?v=QVeZ68Ks7-4

★ *Metal/Frosted Translucent Business Cards*
CONCEPT: To make an individual or business really stand out, metal or frosted translucent business cards are really effective. They are also a great small business if nobody or few are offering this product in your area. See samples at the websites below.

COMPANY/INVENTOR: Many now but coverage in your area may be thin or non-existent.
FURTHER INFO: www.plasmadesign.co.uk/metalbusinesscards.htm; www.metalcards.com

★ *Customised Dolls Made To Resemble...You!*
CONCEPT: A company in Singapore makes ceramic dolls in the caricatured image of photographs supplied by customers. This is a neat gift novelty that offers a strong point of difference.
COMPANY/INVENTOR: Red Dot Concept
REAL WORLD BIZ: http://store.reddotconcept.com/ceramic-figurines/cat_2.html

★ *Laughter Yoga*
CONCEPT: Yoga where you...laugh! Based on the indisputable axiom that 'laughter is the best medicine', this branch of yoga promotes well-being through a whole lotta laughing. Hard to argue with that. If there aren't classes offered in your area, this small business could be for you.
COMPANY/INVENTOR: Dr Madan Kataria
FURTHER INFO: www.laughteryoga.org

★ *Optical Illusion 'Truckvertising'*
CONCEPT: While advertising on large trucks like 'mobile billboards' has been around for ages, creating clever, striking and engaging optical illusions with those advertising spaces has not. Check the samples on the websites below. What a brilliant way to promote your new small business in your area or as a small business in itself. The trucks also serve as ads for such a brilliant small business.
COMPANY/INVENTOR: Someone I'd like to meet for lunch
FURTHER INFO: www.trendhunter.com/trends/

truckvertising; www.whatatop.com (See 'Advertising' section for some brilliant examples)

★ *'Flying' T-shirt Store*
CONCEPT: A t-shirt store in trendy Brick Lane in London attracts customers by having their t-shirt inventory 'flying' around above their customers' heads on a conveyor belt system. As a line in the section on *Best Business Quotes Of All Time* on Page 63 in this book states: "It's not what you sell that matters. It's how you sell it."
COMPANY/INVENTOR: Illustrated People
FURTHER INFO: www.illustratedpeople.com

★ *Faith Based Weight Loss Church*
CONCEPT: Given that Christian converts are harder to come by these days, one LA church now offers weight loss support along with spiritual guidance.
COMPANY/INVENTOR: Body Temple Wellness
FURTHER INFO: www.bodytemplewellness.com

★ *Art Vending Machine*
CONCEPT: Using 'antique' cigarette vending machines, this company sells small artworks from selected contemporary artists through these units. Perfect for a trendy, alternative area.
COMPANY/INVENTOR: Art-O-Mat
FURTHER INFO: www.artomat.org

★ *Charity Vending Machine*
CONCEPT: Most machines offer a product in return for inserting money. This one offers nothing except a feeling of contribution as you have donated that money to one of the nominated charities on the 'vending' machine. A variation of this machine is that you buy an item and have the option of donating your change to a charity of your

choice from the options available.
COMPANY/INVENTOR: Coinstar, among others.
FURTHER INFO: www.seihin-world.com/s/2006/
05/08_0317.php

★ *Coin-to-Cash Conversion Vending Machine*
CONCEPT: Coins are a nuisance for most people so this machine allows users to bring their change into one of these units and have it converted to notes (via a voucher at the nearby customer service desk, for example) – for about an 8% handling fee. Perfect for a supermarket or mall site.
COMPANY/INVENTOR: Coinstar
FURTHER INFO: www.coinstar.co.uk/uk/html/A1-3-1

★ *LED Light Incapacitator*
CONCEPT: By 'firing' different colors and random pulses at a person e.g. suspected criminals, the target quickly feels disoriented and nauseous. No permanent side effects result from using this defensive device. Mace, move over.
COMPANY/INVENTOR: Intelligent Optical Systems
FURTHER INFO: www.intopsys.com

★ *Sonic Barrier Burglar Alarm*
CONCEPT: Unlike a conventional burglar alarm, the Inferno, from Sweden, makes intruders feel chest pains, vertigo and nausea by generating frequencies at around 125 dB.
COMPANY/INVENTOR: Indusec
FURTHER INFO: www.indusec.com/secprod.html

★ *The SOS Helmet*
CONCEPT: If a lone mountain climber or bike rider wearing the *Wireless Impact Guardian* (WIG?) receives a knock to the head, the helmet starts beeping. If the unit is

not switched off within one minute, the helmet automatically begins transmitting an SOS with the wearer's GPS co-ordinates.
COMPANY/INVENTOR: Brycen Spencer
FURTHER INFO: www.theinfosage.com/news/1337/ article/27661/2008-02-10.html

★ *Traveller Rest/Business Cocoons*
CONCEPT: For business people on the fly or travellers in general, futuristic, cocoon-like 'shells' in airports and public places are a great 'oasis' in which to work, phone, relax or nap. The concept is even spreading *outside* Japan to micro-room hotels like that of Yotel below.
COMPANY/INVENTOR: Nemorelax
FURTHER INFO: www.nemorelax.com; www.yotel.com

★ *DIY Customised Sleeping Bags*
CONCEPT: In attempting to entice buyers with enhanced customisability, one British outdoor gear firm is now offering online buyers up to 17 different sleeping bag designs in a big range of styles depending on bag weight and climate catered for.
COMPANY/INVENTOR: Peter Hutchinson Designs
FURTHER INFO: www.phdesigns.co.uk/ dyosleepingbag/version_choice.htm

★ *The World's Only Stand-Up Fisherman's Kayak?*
CONCEPT: Fishing and kayaking are normally exclusive of each other. However, thanks to the radical design of this new kayak, stable standing on/in a kayak is easy and thus allows fishing from a standing position.
COMPANY/INVENTOR: Via Hammacher Schlemmer
FURTHER INFO: www.hammacher.com/publish/ 11098.asp

★ *'Doctor Fish' Psoriasis Treatment/Fish Reflexology/ Fish Spa*
CONCEPT: In parts of Asia, especially Singapore, the therapeutic use of fish to nibble away dead and dermatologically affected skin is well known. Apparently, the process is very cleansing – even if the hungry fish bites feel like tiny electric shocks as they happily go about their work. With a big Asian population across the Western world, there's nothing fishy about bringing this small business to the West.
COMPANY/INVENTOR: Unknown
FURTHER INFO: www.chinadaily.com.cn/lifestyle/ 2007-01/18/content_786913.htm; http://uk.youtube.com/watch?v=sYnU3dgF3do

★ *Portable Planetarium*
CONCEPT: Planetariums have been with us for a long time. They are a fun and engaging way to learn about space. Yet, until now, that ability has not been available in the home. With a display of some 10,000 stars, this portable home plantarium makes an exceptional and unique gift or entertaining social prop at home.
COMPANY/INVENTOR: Segatoys (among others)
FURTHER INFO: http://toys.brando.com.hk/ prod_detail.php?prod_id=00109

★ *Fashion Laptop Carry Cases*
CONCEPT: Virtually all laptops/notebooks are only available with a dull, black nylon corporate carry case. For women though, fashionable alternatives are starting to appear and are already proving popular.
COMPANY/INVENTOR: Abbi (among others)
FURTHER INFO: www.abbinewyork.com; www.ecasewarehouse.com (they do a nice denim carry case too)

★ *The Waboba Ball*
CONCEPT: Intended as a recreational beach and park replacement for Frisbees, volleyballs, soccer balls et al, the British *Waboba Ball* – about the size of a tennis ball - is made of lycra and bounces well on water.
COMPANY/INVENTOR: Waboba International
FURTHER INFO: www.waboba.com; http://uk.youtube.com/watch?v=roeEZi5I32w

★ *Hydrogen-Powered Remote Controlled Car*
CONCEPT: At some point, it was probably inevitable that the eco-revolution we are now firmly in the grip of would filter down to things like...remote control cars, such as the *H2GO* powered by a hydrogen fuel cell. Are these available in your area yet?
COMPANY/INVENTOR: Corgi
FURTHER INFO: www.corgi.biz/h2go/index.html

★ *Floating/Hovering Lounge Chair*
CONCEPT: Powered by magnetic fields, this unique lounge chair, the *Lounger*, hovers above the floor thanks to powerful repellent magnets beneath it. However, the *Lounger* doesn't agree with credit cards or pacemakers!
COMPANY/INVENTOR: Keith Dixon
FURTHER INFO: http://uk.youtube.com/watch?v=drfEF0c2nh0; www.lucitesolutions.com/casestudy.cfm?action=casestudy_view&id=1425

★ *Solar Charging Backpack*
CONCEPT: Given that backpacks are constantly exposed to sunlight while outdoors, making them a storage unit for solar energy seems logical. This unit can generate up to 4 watts of power – enough for recharging small handheld devices such as MP3 players, PDAs et al.
COMPANY/INVENTOR: Voltaic
FURTHER INFO: www.voltaicsystems.com/

bag_converter.shtml

★ *Collapsible Catamaran* (that can fit under a bed!)
CONCEPT: The *Smartkat* is a collapsible boat from Austria that weighs just 39 kilograms, takes 20 minutes to assemble without tools and fits in two 180 x 30 x 30 centimeter bags.
COMPANY/INVENTOR: Smartkat GmbH
FURTHER INFO: www.smartkat.at/en_smartkat.html

★ *Elderly-Friendly Smart Carpet*
CONCEPT: Thanks to this technologically-oriented new carpet in development, elderly people living alone can get help if they suffer a fall at home. If they do fall, a nominated caregiver is automatically notified with a warning message.
COMPANY/INVENTOR: Harry Tyrer/University of Missouri
FURTHER INFO: Contact the University of Missouri

★ *Super-Light 'Aircraft'* (that also travels on land and water)
CONCEPT: At just 60 kilograms, the Russian *Evolution* is a futuristic, one-man, flying machine built mainly of kevlar. Given its Kevlar and plastic body, the *Evolution* is also invisible to radar and has a parachute system if it gets into mechanical trouble.
COMPANY/INVENTOR: Alexander Begak
FURTHER INFO: http://english.pravda.ru/science/tech/31-01-2008/103775-russian_designer-0

★ *Wearable Airbag For Motorcyclists*
CONCEPT: The *D-Air* system is a part of a specialised motorcycle jacket that deploys in 40 milliseconds when it senses that the rider is falling. Such a technology seems likely to become mandatory for all motorcyclists to wear

given the legal necessity of cars to have airbags since 1989 in the US.
COMPANY/INVENTOR: Dainese
FURTHER INFO: http://uk.youtube.com/watch?v=ojT9ogxeW84; www.dainese.com/eng/d-air.asp

★ *Quiet Power-Generating Wind Turbine*
CONCEPT: The *quietrevolution* is a new innovation in windmill/turbine design from Britain that is smaller (5 metres high), quieter and more capable of handling changing wind directions. It even looks good.
COMPANY/INVENTOR: quietrevolution ltd
FURTHER INFO: www.quietrevolution.co.uk

★ *'Eco-Luxury' Laundry/Dry Cleaning*
CONCEPT: In return for a set weekly fee, one New York laundry service offers well-heeled clients a premium service with scheduled pick-up times and the comfort that expensive clothes will be treated with TLC using the most eco-friendly washing materials presently available.
COMPANY/INVENTOR: Slate NYC
FURTHER INFO: www.slatenyc.com

★ *'Kiddo Kidkeeper' Proximity Alarm for Parents*
CONCEPT: The *Kiddo Kidkeeper* wireless proximity alarm from Portugal alerts parents or carers when a child under their supervision is about to leave a specified spatial zone. The manufacturer calls it a 'virtual fence' and it can offer real peace of mind in an age where fear of child abduction or negligence is common. Shockingly, some 800,000 children disappear in America every year (National Center for Missing and Exploited Children).
COMPANY/INVENTOR: Smart Target (*Aerotel GeoSkeeper* and *Skeeper* from Israel at www.aerotel.com/en/products-solutions/lifecare-mobile-solutions/

geoskeeper.html are similar products)
FURTHER INFO: www.smart-target.pt/
index.php ?lingua=en

★ *Home Hydrogen Power Generator*
CONCEPT: According to this innovative British
company, their electrolyser uses renewable energy
sources to create hydrogen fuel that can then utilised for
central heating and cooking. From this system, no carbon
emissions are produced.
COMPANY/INVENTOR: ITM Power
FURTHER INFO: www.itm-power.com

★ *'PalmPeeler' Intuitive Vegetable Peeler*
CONCEPT: Designed as a kind of 'hand extension', the
PalmPeeler offers a much easier vegetable peeling
experience than conventional peelers of the past.
COMPANY/INVENTOR: Chef'n Corporation (check
out their range of other clever kitchen devices too)
FURTHER INFO: www.chefn.com/products/
gadgets/palm_peeler.html

★ *Vocal Smoke Alarm*
CONCEPT: Unlike conventional 'whistling' smoke
alarms, the *SignalONE Safety Vocal Smoke Alarm* is
presently the only alarm that allows a parent or carer to
record an emergency vocal message. Research suggests
that this is more effective than smoke alarm tones.
COMPANY/INVENTOR: Signalonesafety
FURTHER INFO: www.signalonesafety.com

★ *BioKnob Home Biometric Door Lock*
CONCEPT: Replacing conventional locks and keys, the
BioKnob can store the biometric identities of up to 1000
users and can easily add and delete the data of temporary
guests.

COMPANY/INVENTOR: Tychi Systems
FURTHER INFO: www.tychisystems.com/products.asp

★ *Log Home Building Classes*
CONCEPT: The Log Home Builder's Association of North America provides 2-day classes on building log homes. These are very popular and demonstrate that building a log cabin on land in the right location or simply teaching or organizing the teaching of classes with hired tutors can be very profitable.
COMPANY/INVENTOR: LHBA
FURTHER INFO: www.loghomebuilders.org

★ *'To-Do Tattoos'*
CONCEPT: Most of us have a mental or actual 'To Do' list these days as our lives get busier. This clever development playfully works off that fact with its temporary 'To Do' tattoo list. Don't forget it.
COMPANY/INVENTOR: Via Fred & Friends
FURTHER INFO: www.worldwidefred.com/todotattoo.htm

★ *'Clocky' Evasive Alarm Clock*
CONCEPT: Clocky, a fiendish, wheel-footed alarm clock, sounds off and then scurries around your room so you have to wake up, get out of bed, find him, turn the alarm off and then kill him. Nasty.
COMPANY/INVENTOR: Gauri Nanda
FURTHER INFO: www.nandahome.com

★ *'Looj' Remote Control Roof Gutter Cleaning Robot*
CONCEPT: The remote control *Looj* robot attempts to make gutter cleaning – a necessary chore – safer, faster and less hassle.
COMPANY/INVENTOR: iRobot Corporation (while you're visiting their website, check their vacuum cleaning

robots, floor washing robots, sweeping robots and pool cleaning robots)
FURTHER INFO: www.irobot.com

★ *Transparent Toaster* (Concept Only)
CONCEPT: In another brilliant concept-in-development that capitalizes on consumer boredom, this completely transparent toaster allows users to watch bread toasting right in front of them.
COMPANY/INVENTOR: Via Inventables
FURTHER INFO: www.inventables.com/Product/ConceptStudio.asp?i=11

★ *Remote Control Hybrid Lawnmower*
CONCEPT: Capable of traversing 45-degree inclines, the *Evatech GOAT* can be operated by anyone who can handle a remote control car. Hybrid power ticks another consumer box too.
COMPANY/INVENTOR: Evatech (check out Husqvarna and Zucchetti too at website below)
FURTHER INFO: www.evatech.net (and also check out some cool robotic lawnmowers over at www.robotsandrelax.com)

★ *Anti-Theft iPod Retro Disguise*
CONCEPT: If thieves love iPods, they definitely don't care about ancient old Sony Walkman cassette players. Solution? Create an old Sony Walkman case for a shiny new iPod.
COMPANY/INVENTOR: Via Slipperybrick
FURTHER INFO: www.gadgetvenue.com/ipod-in-disguise-02035558/; www.slipperybrick.com/2008/02/ipod-disguise-walkman/

★ *Luxury Designer Homes For Dogs*
CONCEPT: For the well-heeled looking for something to

spend their money on, why not luxury designer doghouses for their pooches? Also check out dog wash vending over on Page 141 and dog walking on Page 230.
COMPANY/INVENTOR: Marco Morosini
FURTHER INFO: www.lifelounge.com/Luxury-Mobile-Homes-for-Pets.aspx

★ *'GlobalPetFinder' GPS System*
CONCEPT: *GlobalPetFinder* uses a rechargeable GPS tag that can be attached to any collar and relay an animal's location straight to a mobile phone or PDA.
COMPANY/INVENTOR: GPS Tracks
FURTHER INFO: www.globalpetfinder.com

★ *'K9 Kalmer' Dog Quieter*
CONCEPT: Unlike other behavioural modifying devices for pets that rely on pain or irritation to an animal, the *K9 Kalmer* seeks to calm unruly Cujos with "ultrasonic musical compositions".
COMPANY/INVENTOR: Variety International
FURTHER INFO: www.k9kalmer.com

★ *Recyclable Reusable Cardboard Playhouses*
CONCEPT: From Britain comes a range of cool, recyclable, foldable and re-usable cardboard playhouses including toy forts, dolls houses, tepees and rockets.
COMPANY/INVENTOR: Paperpod
FURTHER INFO: www.paperpod.co.uk

★ *Pre-Fab Designer Treehouses*
CONCEPT: These elaborate pre-fab treehouses have to be seen to be believed and any business that targets children successfully today can do very well (look at Australia's *The Wiggles*, for example).
COMPANY/INVENTOR: Daniels Wood Land (among others)

FURTHER INFO: www.danielswoodland.com

★ *The 'Walkodile' Child Safety Walker*
CONCEPT: For any parent or carer supervising more than walking one child is demanding to say the least. To this end, the *Walkodile* from Scotland links together up to 6 children with a flexible spine (see picture at the website below) and makes the task much safer and more manageable.
COMPANY/INVENTOR: Elaine Stephen/Red Island
FURTHER INFO: www.walkodile.com

★ *Image-On-Nails Inkjet Printer*
CONCEPT: The *ImagiNail NailJet Pro* is an inkjet printer capable of printing any image on to nails. That in itself could be a great business opportunity waiting to be developed in your area.
COMPANY/INVENTOR: ImagiNail Holdings
FURTHER INFO: www.imaginail.com

★ *'Firewheel' Rubber Band Machine-gun*
CONCEPT: This toy weapon variation for children (boys?) fires rubber bands in quick succession like, unsurprisingly, a machine-gun.
COMPANY/INVENTOR: Tasman Engineering
FURTHER INFO: www.firewheel.com.au

★ *'Flybar' Pogo Stick*
CONCEPT: Using aircraft-grade aluminium, the *Flybar*, a kind of 21st century pogo stick, can reach heights of 8 feet, according to the manufacturer - thanks to its trampoline-like qualities.
COMPANY/INVENTOR: Andy Macdonald/SBI Enterprises
FURTHER INFO: www.flybar.com/pages/home.html

★ *'Airzooka' Air Bazooka*

CONCEPT: As a variation on other toy 'weapons' for children, the *Airzooka* shoots only air. Live demonstration in front of children to harness their 'pester power' is highly recommended. It also glows in the dark.

COMPANY/INVENTOR: Various sources inc. Firebox below

FURTHER INFO: www.firebox.com/product/ 567?aff=1272

★ *Jelly Click Mouse*

CONCEPT: If you find a computer mouse too hard and unyielding, this *Jelly* mouse could be a winner as it feels floppy and…like jelly.

COMPANY/INVENTOR: Bongkun Shin, Heungkyo Seo, Jiwoong Hwang & Wooteik Lim

FURTHER INFO: www.shinyshiny.tv/2008/02/ jelly_click_inf.html

★ *Moldable Mouse*

CONCEPT: This mouse allows users to mold a computer mouse into the most desirable shape for their hand. Businesses based on a product like this probably need to be based on live demonstration.

COMPANY/INVENTOR: Lite-On

FURTHER INFO: http://dvice.com/archives/2008/ 01/liteon_moldable.php

★ *'Swerver' Quad Skates*

CONCEPT: With a single large wheel on each corner of a skate, this roller skating innovation offers a very different skating experience.

COMPANY/INVENTOR: Inventist (take a look at Inventist's other interesting new products at the website below as well)

FURTHER INFO: www.inventist.com

★ *'AquaSkipper' Water 'Hopper'*
CONCEPT: The *AquaSkipper* is an aquatic hydrofoil device powered only by its rider's hopping action. As such, it can be conceived as both a recreational device and cardiovascular exercise machine.
COMPANY/INVENTOR: AquaSkipper
FURTHER INFO: www.jumpusa.com/ aquaskipper.html

★ *Patting-Activated Dog Lamp*
CONCEPT: As a novel gimmick, this dog-shaped lamp reacts to being 'patted' by switching on the light. Could be a winner with children.
COMPANY/INVENTOR: Via Drinkstuff
FURTHER INFO: www.drinkstuff.com/products/ product.asp?ID=4565

★ *'Spilt' Candles*
CONCEPT: Candles are a great product for a small business as they can be manufactured at home in a variety of customised shapes that add novelty value to an item that has proven appeal with women at market stalls et al. Here, these candles appear to be 'melted' but that is in fact their clever design. See the pictures at the website below.
COMPANY/INVENTOR: Via Drinkstuff
FURTHER INFO: www.dutchbydesign.com/content/ products/products.cfm?Category=Candles&CatID=15

★ *Ultrasonic Jewellery Cleaner*
CONCEPT: Using ultrasonic waves, this device can thoroughly clean jewellery without any manual labor in three minutes. It even works on dentures and DVDs/CDs.
COMPANY/INVENTOR: Via Hammacher Schlemmer
FURTHER INFO: www.hammacher.com/publish/ 74177.asp

★ *Bungee-Powered Backpack*
CONCEPT: In another clever application of physics, this new 'suspended-load ergonomic backpack' can potentially reduce the load of a backpack by up to 86%. That sounds like a load off. Literally and metaphorically.
COMPANY/INVENTOR: Larry Rome/University of Pennsylvania
FURTHER INFO: www.upenn.edu/pennnews/article.php?id=1064

★ *KTRAK Mountain Ski-Bike*
CONCEPT: Basically, it's a Canadian mountain bike with a ski instead of a front wheel and a track looped off the back wheel. It is thus capable of far more manoeuvres than either skis or a mountain bike.
COMPANY/INVENTOR: Ktrakcycle
FURTHER INFO: www.ktrakcycle.com; www.youtube.com/watch?v=5LaUvlnDyyI

★ *Wheeled Snow Shovel*
CONCEPT: Shovelling snow in colder climates is a real chore. However, the *Wovel* uses the laws of physics to make it considerably easier – up to 80% easier according to the manufacturer.
COMPANY/INVENTOR: Structured Solutions II
FURTHER INFO: http://wovel.com/

★ *Quiet Leaf Blower*
CONCEPT: Solving an obvious noise problem, this quiet leaf blower could offer small lawn care businesses using the *356BT Quiet Blower* a nice advantage over noisier rivals.
COMPANY/INVENTOR: Husqvarna
FURTHER INFO: www.usa.husqvarna.com/products_homeowner_product_details.aspx?pid=1181

★ *LifeLocator 'Personfinder'*
CONCEPT: In certain emergency situations such as fires, landslides, earthquakes, avalanches and other disasters, finding people buried alive is obviously very important. Using ultra wideband technology, the *LifeLocator* can locate human beings 15-20 feet from the sensor through debris. Shouldn't every emergency worker in the world have this device?
COMPANY/INVENTOR: UltraVision
FURTHER INFO: www.ultravisionsecurity.com

★ *'Yelpie' Portable Outdoor Lightweight Personal Safe*
CONCEPT: If you are at the beach and want to go swimming, how do you make sure that your wallet/keys/purse/stuff isn't stolen while you're in the water? Easy. You use an Australian shoebox-sized *Yelpie* portable safe that lets off a loud alarm if any unauthorised movement takes place.
COMPANY/INVENTOR: Yelpie Pty Ltd (Also check out the *Mooncode Safe* @ www.boysstuff.co.uk)
FURTHER INFO: www.yelpie.com

★ *Chocolate Tool Set*
CONCEPT: In a perfect illustration of customising an existing product to attract consumer interest, this set of *Automania* men's tools made of chocolate from Japan makes a fantastic gift for Father's Day, birthdays, Christmas et al.
COMPANY/INVENTOR: Frantz
FURTHER INFO: www.techchee.com/2008/02/14/automania-bolts-and-nuts-chocolate-set-melts-diyers-heart-on-valentines-day/

★ *Personal Lightning Detector*
CONCEPT: *StrikeAlert* is a small, pager-sized lightning detector that is capable of detecting lightning up to 70

kilometres away. It can also indicate the direction that the lightning is travelling. Perfect for outdoor- types as around 10,000 people are killed by lightning each year across the world.
COMPANY/INVENTOR: Outdoors Technologies
FURTHER INFO: www.strikealert.com

★ *Wristwatch Fish Finder*
CONCEPT: This sonar fish finding device is worn on the wrist and communicates with a sensor on the end of the fishing line. The *Humminbird Smartcast RF30* scans a radius of 25 meters and gives an impression of the sea floor below and anything on it. How 21st century is that?
COMPANY/INVENTOR: Via Boating's Leading Accessories
FURTHER INFO: www.humminbird.com.au

★ *Flickable Food Fight Cutlery Weapons*
CONCEPT: Perfect for children and selling at markets where demonstrations are possible, the flickable Zing cutlery looks promising. If you're not the one covered in food.
COMPANY/INVENTOR: Via Fred & Friends
FURTHER INFO: www.worldwidefred.com/zing.htm

★ *Retro Wooden Radios*
CONCEPT: Cashing in on retro isn't new but it can be profitable. The *Magno* wooden radio contains a conventional modern MP3-compatible radio inside but looks like a real furniture item. This trend is cropping up with computer monitors, steres and TVs too.
COMPANY/INVENTOR: Via Uncrate
FURTHER INFO: http://www.uncrate.com/men/gear/home-audio-speakers/magno-wooden-radio/

★ *Gelaskins iPod/Mobile/Laptop 'Skins'*

CONCEPT: It has not taken long for the ubiquitous iPod to encourage spinoff products, some of which we have included in this book. These varied, imaginative Canadian 'skins' allow iPod users to customise and conceal their beloved music player or other portable device and show how a simple, lateral idea is easily possible. *Gelaskins* are available for laptops too.
COMPANY/INVENTOR: GelaSkins Inc
FURTHER INFO: www.gelaskins.com

★ *Voodoo Knife Block*

CONCEPT: For those with a darker sense of humor, the *Voodoo Knife Block* features a standing figure where the kitchen knives sit as though he/she has been stabbed with them. Dark but funny and great for a market stall. See the picture below.
COMPANY/INVENTOR: Raffaele Iannello
FURTHER INFO: www.voodooknifeblock.co.uk

★ *LED T-Shirts That Light Up*

CONCEPT: The *T-Equaliser* and *TQ-Heart* t-shirts feature embedded LED lights into their front – either a stereo graphic equaliser or a giant heart. The *T-Equaliser* responds to music around the wearer while the *TQ-Heart* lights up as two wearers approach each other. Light levels increase until they peak when the wearers are closest. Great for lovers and/or clubbing. Also perfect for a market stall with live demonstrations.
COMPANY/INVENTOR: Via Firebox
FURTHER INFO: www.uk-shopping-mall.com/cgi-bin/ESsmproduct.cgi?id=6960721

★ *Customisable 'My Monopoly'*

CONCEPT: *My Monopoly* offers buyers the ability to buy a Monopoly game where the names of the properties

have actually been chosen by the purchaser e.g. Maria's Brother's Dump instead of Mayfair.
COMPANY/INVENTOR: Hasbro
FURTHER INFO: www.mymonopoly.com/home.php

★ *The Beerbelly Stealth Drink Vessel*
CONCEPT: When worn under clothes, the *Beerbelly* simply makes the wearer appear a little tubby. However, inside the *Beerbelly* is a secret cavity where beer (or another fluid) can be stored and accessed through a hidden straw.
COMPANY/INVENTOR: Under Development Inc
FURTHER INFO: www.thebeerbelly.com

★ *Despair Calendar/Despair T-Shirts*
CONCEPT: Cleverly creating difference from the conventional, these products offer cynical and downbeat slogans on t-shirts and *Demotivators* calendars that humorously mock inspiring products elsewhere e.g. "If you're not part of the solution, there's good money to be made prolonging the problem."
COMPANY/INVENTOR: Despair Inc
FURTHER INFO: www.despair.com

★ *Miss Army Knife – The Female Swiss Army Knife* (a.k.a. *Miss A Kit*)
CONCEPT: Brilliant name and product. Designed for women, the *Miss Army Knife*, like its iconic male counterpart, features a range of tools in one utility device except for female use. Tools on the *Miss Army Knife* include tweezers, nail file, safety pin and corkscrew.
COMPANY/INVENTOR: Missakit
FURTHER INFO: www.missakit.com

★ *'Orgasmatron' Head Massager*
CONCEPT: Another great product for a market stall

with live demonstrations – a home head massager. Though not necessarily orgasmic, the Australian *Orgasmatron* is still very pleasurable despite its spooky, spidery, claw-like appearance. There is a vibrating version too.

COMPANY/INVENTOR: Dwayne Lacey
FURTHER INFO: www.orgasmatron.com.au

★ *Fold-Up Bike*
CONCEPT: As an urban commuter solution, the British *A-bike* takes some beating – a bicycle weighing less than 6 kilograms that can be folded into a carry bag. Plus, all cables and chains are internal within its aluminium frame. The website below has a cool video of the *A-bike* in action.

COMPANY/INVENTOR: Clive Sinclair
FURTHER INFO: www.a-bike.co.uk

★ *Optical Illusions in Various Forms*
CONCEPT: Grand Illusions, a canny British firm, offer a stunning range of optical illusion products that have to be seen - via videos on their website - to be believed. Very impressive. Their regular toys and products are pretty cool too.

COMPANY/INVENTOR: Grand Illusions
FURTHER INFO: www.grand-illusions.com

★ *'Kayacht' Powered Kayak*
CONCEPT: The *Kayacht* is a normal looking kayak with the added benefit of an electronic motor that can provide up to 4 hours of additional propulsion. It also has solar panels for additional energy.

COMPANY/INVENTOR: Kayacht Electric Boats
FURTHER INFO: www.kayacht.com

★ *Halitosis (Bad Breath) Detector*
CONCEPT: Arguably an essential accessory in the competitive world of dating, this innovative device could avoid a humiliating 'oral malfunction'.
COMPANY/INVENTOR: Tanita
FURTHER INFO: http://dvice.com/archives/ 2008/02/halitosis_detec.php; www.geeksugar.com/ 1009155 (see consumer feedback on it there too)

★ *Modular Fish Tank*
CONCEPT: In a visually interesting alternative to the rectangular home aquarium, this new product, the *Silverfish Aquarium*, features inter-connected bulbous tanks that the fish can swim between.
COMPANY/INVENTOR: Octopus Studios
FURTHER INFO: www.octopusstudios.com

★ *Rolling Park Bench*
CONCEPT: In public spaces, park benches can become wet or home to the homeless. This Korean rotating bench solves both of those issues. The rolling part can be easily replaced when it becomes dirty too. Has your local council/government heard about them yet?
COMPANY/INVENTOR: Sungwoo Park
FURTHER INFO: www.coroflot.com

★ *Marshmallow Blaster/Marshmallow Blower*
CONCEPT: Another wacky toy from the brilliant nuts at Stupid.com that boys will love. Set this candy bazooka up at a market stall with ongoing demonstrations and watch these babies sell!
COMPANY/INVENTOR: Stupid.com
FURTHER INFO: www.stupid.com/stat/MLLW.html

★ *Glowing Bicycle*
CONCEPT: Typical of creating a fusion of fashion,

advanced safety and old-school technology, a leading sportswear manufacturer has developed a neon-style glowing bicycle, the *Glow Rider*. The best thing about a product like this is that it advertises itself and attracts attention wherever the user goes – (free) marketing like this does not get any more cost-effective.
COMPANY/INVENTOR: Puma
FURTHER INFO: www.treehugger.com/files/2008/01/glow_in_the_dar.php

★ *Motorcycle Chopper Inspired Pizza-Cutters*
CONCEPT: Ideas like this variation on a pizza cutter brilliantly tackle a massive consumer dynamic: boredom. Any small business that can an add an element of novelty to an everyday item can do very well with today's innovation/gimmick-hungry consumer.
COMPANY/INVENTOR: Frankie Flood
FURTHER INFO: Museum of Wisconsin Art

★ *USB Missile Launcher*
CONCEPT: For the children at home and the adult-sized children at the office, the *USB* (Foam) *Missile Launcher*, complete with sound effects and a built-in webcam to watch its trajectory in first person, is another USB-powered spinoff but is just the kind of fun widget that can sell well.
COMPANY/INVENTOR: Via I Want One Of Those (See other nifty products there too)
FURTHER INFO: www.iwantoneofthose.com/office-toys/web-cam-missile-launcher/index.html

★ *Paper Scales*
CONCEPT: These are bathroom scales that function normally except that it is made out of...paper? It's very thin, waterproof and can even be rolled up for storage.
COMPANY/INVENTOR: Duck Image Studio

FURTHER INFO: www.gizmowatch.com/entry/paper-scale-from-duck-image-studio/

★ *Power Usage 'Saverclip'*
CONCEPT: This ingenious device simply clips on to any power cord and instantly displays the amount of power that is being used on that line. The *Saverclip* even recharges itself from the electromagnetic fields that it is monitoring.
COMPANY/INVENTOR: Tsunho Wang, Insu Wang, Jongheui Lee, Youngdon Lee
FURTHER INFO: www.gigodo.com/saverclip-reveals-your-energy-usage.html

★ *Collapsible Surfboard*
CONCEPT: For surfers living in a confined space or who travel a great deal, especially by air, having a collapsible surfboard could be very practical. Roof racks on a car are no longer necessary for surfboards either.
COMPANY/INVENTOR: Nicholas Notara
FURTHER INFO: www.gadgettastic.com/2008/02/13/collapsible-surf-board/

★ *Pillows/Cushions That Look Like Rocks*
CONCEPT: This French innovation is a great talking point in your lounge – cushions and pillows that look like rocks from a mountain stream. Just like real rocks, they come in different sizes and look fantastic – check out the pictures at the website below.
COMPANY/INVENTOR: Livingstones
FURTHER INFO: www.gearfuse.com/jump-into-a-comfy-pile-of-stones/

★ *Gravity Powered LED Floor Lamp*
CONCEPT: Apparently, gravity can be used as a source of energy. Who knew? This inventor did and his device

uses gravity to feed energy to 10 LEDs inside a floor lamp. No cords. Just move a weight from the bottom of the elegant lamp to the top and it's got power.
COMPANY/INVENTOR: Clay Moulton
FURTHER INFO: www.vtnews.vt.edu/ story.php?relyear=2008&itemno=111

★ *Self-Balancing Tray*
CONCEPT: Every restaurant and club in the world should have these revolutionary trays. They allow staff to only need one hand to safely carry a tray, thus leaving the other hand to serve. When the tray is swung around, the drinks still remain stable. Counter-balancing physics, it seems, is pretty cool after all. See the pictures below to get the idea.
COMPANY/INVENTOR: Gijs Bakker
FURTHER INFO: www.pedlars.co.uk/page_1023.html; www.betterlivingthroughdesign.com/2007/12/selfbalanc ing_tray.html:

★ *Pick Your Nose Cups*
CONCEPT: For children or parties, these disposable cups have a range of comical noses pictured on their side so that someone drinking from that cup looks like they have that nose (and moustache) in some cases. Fun.
COMPANY/INVENTOR: Some nosy person
FURTHER INFO: www.dailycandy.com/everywhere/ article/30115/Follow+Your+Nose; www.lazyboneuk.com /store/pro799.html

★ *Smoke Ring Gun*
CONCEPT: The *Zero Blaster* should appeal to boys who've tired of water pistols and the like. At market stalls, innovative products like this one do well as children can see them in action and thus use their 'pester power' to influence parents to buy. Like some other interesting new

products listed here which could quickly translate into a market-sited small business, www.Stupid.com (featured on our Recommended website list on Page 259) has many brilliant, child-oriented products available.

COMPANY/INVENTOR: Stupid.com
FURTHER INFO: www.stupid.com/stat/ZERB.html

★ *Upside-Down Tomato Garden*
CONCEPT: By inverting the garden, this clever set-up creates a virtually maintenance free indoor/outdoor tomato garden.
COMPANY/INVENTOR: Hammacher Schlemmer (their other innovative products are well worth checking out on their website too)
FURTHER INFO: www.hammacher.com/publish/67403.asp

★ *Nose Pencil Sharpener*
CONCEPT: A typically gross product from Stupid.com that children will love. Insert the pencil up the plastic nostril and sharpen away. Nice.
COMPANY/INVENTOR: Stupid.com
FURTHER INFO: www.stupid.com/stat/NOPE.html

★ *Synthetic Wishbones*
CONCEPT: This Seattle company have solved the issue - was it an issue? - of having enough wishbones to snap at the holiday dinner table. Sold in multiple packs, everybody can make a wish with these synthetic wishbones.
COMPANY/INVENTOR: Lucky Break Wishbone Corp
FURTHER INFO: www.luckybreakwishbone.com

★ *Glamor Model Caddies*
CONCEPT: Like the bikini/body builder car wash, Eye Candy Caddies, provides attractive women as caddies for

golfers. Sex, in everything it still seems, sells.
COMPANY/INVENTOR: Eye Candy Caddies
FURTHER INFO: www.eyecandycaddies.com

★ *Online Personal Assistant (PA)*
CONCEPT: Everything else is moving online so why not PA services to help get your crowded professional and personal life sorted?
COMPANY/INVENTOR: Sunday LLC
FURTHER INFO: www.asksunday.com

★ *Personalized Birthday Newspaper*
CONCEPT: Here's a novel birthday gift: a customised newspaper 'front page' celebrating the year of the recipient's year of birth.
COMPANY/INVENTOR: Via Creative Thoughts
FURTHER INFO: http://creativethoughts.net/birthdaychronicle.htm

★ *Inflatable Sumo Costume*
CONCEPT: Memorable from one of the Austin Powers films (who can remember which one?), the inflatable sumo costume is a fun novelty for markets where the impulse buying of children and immature adults makes many small businesses profitable. Could be a great fancy dress costume too!
COMPANY/INVENTOR: Via Boys Stuff UK (Check out their full range of childish chattels)
FURTHER INFO: www.boysstuff.co.uk

★ *Your Photo As Pop Art/Magazine Cover*
CONCEPT: More for the 'left-field' gift folder, myDaVinci, an Illinois-based graphics company, can take a person's photograph and turn it into a variety of stylised portraits or mementoes. Personalization Mall offer a similar cool service with a mocked-up magazine cover.

COMPANY/INVENTOR: myDaVinci, Personalization Mall (many personalized products there)
FURTHER INFO: www.myDaVinci.com; www.personalizationmall.com

★ *Dale Jarrett NASCAR Racing 3 Lap Ride Gift/Experience*
CONCEPT: Like the British company, prezzybox, featured over on Page 189 of this book, Dale Jarrett Racing School offers laps in actual NASCAR cars on NASCAR tracks with racing drivers. Costs vary widely depending on the number of laps desired. Great as a one-off experience or gift. The perfect gift for a car-mad dad on his birthday perhaps?
COMPANY/INVENTOR: Dale Jarrett Racing School
FURTHER INFO: www.racingadventure.com

★ *Fake Fireflies In A Jar*
CONCEPT: This clever illusion could prove engaging for children - glowing 'fireflies' seemingly illuminating a jar. Perfect, like many of these types of novelty products, for a market stall.
COMPANY/INVENTOR: Via Signals (Check out all their cool new products)
FURTHER INFO: www.signals.com (See 'Home & Garden' area)

★ *Automated Wooden Drummer Kit*
CONCEPT: This is an 'old school' - but enticing - style novelty whereby a wooden, mechanical playing drummer that stands (sits?) 9" high made of wood can be assembled by a child. Check out the photo on the website below. A market stall winner.
COMPANY/INVENTOR: Via Signals (Check out all their offbeat products)
FURTHER INFO: www.signals.com/signals/

Gifts_1DA.html

★ *Wearable LED Rainbow Pocket Plasma*
CONCEPT: Children love novelty fashion items - remember 'Scratch & Sniff' or Hypercolor T-shirts? Here, it's a clip-on, wearable *Rainbow Pocket Plasma* with 'crackling' random light patterns. Search the Edmunds site below with "Rainbow Pocket Plasma" to get an eyeful.
COMPANY/INVENTOR: Via Edmund Scientific's (They have plenty of neat stuff there for your next market stall)
FURTHER INFO: http://scientificsonline.com

★ *Remote Control Tarantula*
CONCEPT: Just about ideal for mischievous boys, this RC tarantula has to be a market stall winner.
COMPANY/INVENTOR: Via Spilsbury
FURTHER INFO: www.spilsbury.com

★ *Antquarium*
CONCEPT: Apparently developed by NASA for zero G experiments, the gelatinous material inside this 'aquarium' is a perfect home and food for...ants. Not a bad small business product considering how many original ant farms were sold to an earlier generation. After all, how many times has the yo-yo made a comeback?
COMPANY/INVENTOR: NASA (?)
FURTHER INFO: www.discoverthis.com

★ *Sphereing*
CONCEPT: Sphereing is rolling down hills inside giant, translucent plastic balls. Sphereing can be done alone or in the company of a fellow spherer. All that is needed for this small business is a suitable sphere, a hill and paying customers. Could a small business be any simpler?

Sphering comes in Harness and Aqua flavours too.
COMPANY/INVENTOR: Unknown
FURTHER INFO: www.spheremania.com;
www.intotheblue.co.uk (big range of experiences offered)
www.buyagift.co.uk/Category/Id/1051/Name/Sphereing;

★ *Shark Diving Experiences*
CONCEPT: An exciting variation on charter boat trips is
the novel idea of feeding paying customers in SCUBA
gear to hungry sharks. Admittedly the sharks do have to
work a little at their meal by peeling away underwater
steel cages. This attraction is also available in certain big
aquariums (Manly in Sydney, Australia, for example)
where the sharks are slightly tamer. You may need the
services of the new *Shark Shield* back on Page 89.
COMPANY/INVENTOR: Unknown but dangerous
FURTHER INFO: www.greatwhiteadventures.com;
www.incredible-adventures.com/sharks_farallons.html;
www.sharkdiver.com; www.seesharks.com;
www.excitations.com

★ *Artificial Jellyfish Aquarium*
CONCEPT: If pet fish really get on your nerves with
their constant demands for food and a clean tank, you
may not be alone. The solution? Artificial jellyfish
illuminated by sparkling LED lights of course a.k.a. *The
Moving Jellyfish Lamp.*
COMPANY/INVENTOR: An ichthyophobic inventor
FURTHER INFO: www.boysstuff.co.uk

★ *Five Ferraris Day Drive Experience*
CONCEPT: One British company, I Want One Of Those,
offers the opportunity to drive five (naturally) different
Ferrari sports cars around for a day through the beautiful
Hertfordshire area of England. They call it the *Open
Road Ferrari Sports Car Experience.* Perfect as a gift or

one-off experience. Expensive to set up though - unless the Ferraris are stolen of course!
COMPANY/INVENTOR: I Want One Of Those (They also offer other experiences for car nuts too e.g. *Ferrari Vs Porsche Experience, Lamborghini & Hummer Experience, Aston Martin DB9 Experience*)
FURTHER INFO: www.iwantoneofthose.com

★ *'Bicygnals' Bicycle Indicators*
CONCEPT: In a noble effort to improve cycling safety, *Bicygnals* are motorcycle-style indicators for bicycles. Frankly, these should be legally mandatory.
COMPANY/INVENTOR: Via Be Seen On A Bike
FURTHER INFO: www.beseenonabike.com

★ *Wind-Powered Outdoor Lighting*
CONCEPT: The aptly-named *Firewinder* from Britain is an outdoor light powered by the wind through 14 LEDs, capable of illumination with wind of only 3 mph.
COMPANY/INVENTOR: The Firewinder Company
FURTHER INFO: www.firewinder.com

★ *Extra Room On Wall Outside Your Apartment (?)*
CONCEPT: Now this is too much. You don't like your cramped German apartment or flat so you design, build and attach a whole extra big room on the outside wall of your apartment building that's (securely?) suspended by cables. It's just crazy. Loco. Madness. Or is it? Check out the photos and story below on the websites.
COMPANY/INVENTOR: Stefan Eberstadt
FURTHER INFO: www.convertiblecity.de/ projekte_en.html; http://freshome.com/2008/03/ 03/add-an-additional-room-to-your-apartment/

★ *Wave Propelled Boat*
CONCEPT: Japanese inventor Yutaka Terao loves

sailing but seems less keen on motor-powered marine motion. So he's come up with a 5-knot capable system that powers his beloved 'Suntory Mermaid II' using nothing but energy from the waves using "dolphin like kicks".

COMPANY/INVENTOR: Yutaka Terao
FURTHER INFO: www.tsuneishi.co.jp/english/horie/index.html

★ *Philips Lumalive Textile Garments*
CONCEPT: Dutch electronics giant Philips has unveiled pretty cool new LED-based clothing called Lumalive. Check out the pics at the website below.
COMPANY/INVENTOR: Philips Research
FURTHER INFO: www.newlaunches.com/archives/philips_lumalive_textile_garments.php

★ *Home Kitchen Composter*
CONCEPT: Composters are old school right? Sure. But if they use contemporary styling, technology and tap into eco-consciousness, that's different. The *NatureMill Pro Indoor Composter* functions like a type of trash compactor. By combining, heat, moisture and air flow, compost is created.
COMPANY/INVENTOR: Nature Mill (though other new-tech composters are also available on a Clusty/Google search)
FURTHER INFO: www.naturemill.com

★ *DIY Neon Signs*
CONCEPT: Using snap-on letters kind of like Lego, this home neon sign kit allows any words or phrases to be created in neon.
COMPANY/INVENTOR: Via ThinkGeek
FURTHER INFO: www.thinkgeek.com/gadgets/lights/97fd/

★ *Caffeine Lollipops*
CONCEPT: About time! Not intended for children, these caffeine lollipops, *Javapops*, come in 5 different flavours and pack a 60mg caffeine punch in each one.
COMPANY/INVENTOR: Someone really inspiring
FURTHER INFO: http://caffeinating.blogspot.com/ 2008/02/javapops.html; www.kaboodle.com/reviews/ javapops

★ *'Magic' Wheelchair*
CONCEPT: By introducing new technologies to the ubiquitous wheelchair, *Magicwheels*, is a physics-bending device from Seattle that can be fitted to existing manual wheelchairs and is able to significantly reduce the physical effort required to move a wheel chair while enhancing personal safety.
COMPANY/INVENTOR: Magic Wheels Inc
FURTHER INFO: www.magicwheels.com

★ *Sex Dolls for Dogs*
CONCEPT: OK bear with us. If you are tired of having your pets 'expressing themselves' on your leg or visitors' legs, this innovation can help your frustrated pets release some of that pent-up frustration. Seriously.
COMPANY/INVENTOR: Clement Eloy
FURTHER INFO: www.feeladdicted.com (See 'Life' Section)

★ *USB Digital Microscope*
CONCEPT: Every day, new USB inventions appear. Some are brilliant. Others are just...interesting. This USB-powered 200x microscope has commercial potential, especially given children's love of looking at things through a microscope. Plus, the images through the microscope can be seen on the PC via the USB connection.

COMPANY/INVENTOR: Various
FURTHER INFO: www.paxcam.com;
www.thinkgeek.com/gadgets/electronic/923a/

★ *Inkless Pen That Never Runs Out*
CONCEPT: Based on a metal alloy nib rather than silver, this ingenious pen never needs refilling and leaves unerasable 'pencil-like' writing. It may never run out but it can be lost just like any other pen.
COMPANY/INVENTOR: Via Grand Illusions
FURTHER INFO: www.grand-illusions.com/acatalog/
Metal_Pen.html

★ *Power Popper Ball Launcher*
CONCEPT: Fresh from the Toy Pentagon, this ball-firing weapon comes in two configurations: single barrel and double. No doubt which will be the biggest seller among children out of those two. Brilliant for markets with live demonstrations.
COMPANY/INVENTOR: Unknown
FURTHER INFO: www.thinkgeek.com/geektoys/
warfare/a080/

★ *Elastic Bookshelf*
CONCEPT: This clever Italian invention involves looping a kind of belt that can be stretched around pegs in a variety of potential configurations. It looks brilliant and requires no hammers, nails, bruised thumbs or expletives to change around.
COMPANY/INVENTOR: Arianna Vivenzio
FURTHER INFO: www.ariannavivenzio.com

★ *Ultrasonic Cleaner*
CONCEPT: The *Kumazaki Ultrasonic Cleaner* appears to have a pathological hatred of dirty clothes. That's a good thing. Using sound instead of the world's rapidly

depleting supply of elbow grease, this vicious device blasts away fashion filth with nothing but silent noise.
COMPANY/INVENTOR: Kumazaki
FURTHER INFO: www.bearmax.jp (Japanese language site)

★ *Panda Staple-less Stapler*
CONCEPT: When it comes to binding pages together, *StitchLock Panda's* mantra is, 'why staple when you can stitch?' That way, documents can be easily shredded without the need for staple removal first.
COMPANY/INVENTOR: Via Jbox
FURTHER INFO: www.jbox.com/product/STA314

★ *Oceanic Room Light*
CONCEPT: The somewhat unsexily named *Room Palette Effect Lamp* projects gentle wave motion on to a room's ceiling. It relaxes. It entertains. It soothes. Unless you hate the sea.
COMPANY/INVENTOR: Relaxstyle
FURTHER INFO: http://www.kilian-nakamura.com/catalog/room-palette-effect-lamp-relaxstyle-p-59.html

★ *Car Crash Evidence Video Recorder*
CONCEPT: This mobile video recorder, the *Car Camera Recorder Pro*, features a 2 ½" LCD screen, records everything in front of a car via a camera-equipped rear-view mirror. It is activated automatically when the engine is turned on and switches off when the engine goes off. All video is saved on an SD card so it can be overwritten constantly. Such video evidence is very useful in the event of an accident.
COMPANY/INVENTOR: Via Brickhouse Security
FURTHER INFO: www.brickhousesecurity.com/car-camera-recorder.html

★ *Jet Ski Convertible Boat*
CONCEPT: Like a docking station for a laptop, the *Waveboat* can be secured to a Yamaha Waverunner Jet Ski to convert it into a full-sized boat. Nifty.
COMPANY/INVENTOR: Fun Factory/Yelo Marine
FURTHER INFO: www.fun-f.com

★ *Virtual Ant Farm*
CONCEPT: Actual miniature ant farms were a smash hit with children in the past. This new Tamagotchi though is all virtual.
COMPANY/INVENTOR: Via Japan Trend Shop
FURTHER INFO: www.kilian-nakamura.com/catalog/ants-life-studio-virtual-ant-farm-p-46.html

★ *Hands Free Umbrella*
CONCEPT: Using an offset handle and specially designed shoulder straps, the new *Nubrella* from Florida requires no hands whatsoever - perfect for rainy shopping days.
COMPANY/INVENTOR: Alan Kaufman
FURTHER INFO: www.nubrella.com

★ *Virtual Bubble Wrap With Random Sound*
CONCEPT: Busting the bubbles on bubble wrap is pretty compulsive. Yet this #1 bestseller from the Japan Trend Shop adds in random sounds in a product that simulates the experience of popping sheets of bubblewrap.
COMPANY/INVENTOR: Via Japan Trend Shop
FURTHER INFO: www.kilian-nakamura.com/catalog/index.php

★ *Treetop Adventure Park*
CONCEPT: One way to have loads of fun in the outdoors is to unleash the inner Tarzan in a park specially designed to allow swinging between trees and all manner of walks,

climbs and motion through the trees. One British company, Go Ape, has thus been able to expand to some 16 treetop parks in the last 6 years as its success continues to grow.

COMPANY/INVENTOR: Johnny Weissmuller
FURTHER INFO: www.goape.co.uk; www.adrenalin-forest.co.nz

★ *Glow-In-The-Dark Gravel*
CONCEPT: With a range of obvious safety applications, a Dutch firm has created maintenance-free gravel that glows in the dark. Check the website below for pictures.
COMPANY/INVENTOR: S. Lövenstein BV
FURTHER INFO: http://transmaterial.net (they have a bunch of mad other new stuff too)

★ *Transformer Zippos*
CONCEPT: Sourced from Japan, Zippo lighters with cool *Transformers* (you know, the kids movie and cartoons?) themes are pretty impressive.
COMPANY/INVENTOR: Optimus Prime or his evil counterpart
FURTHER INFO: www.geekologie.com/2008/03/transformer_zippos_have_the_po.php

★ *Sportcopter Super Sport Gyroplane*
CONCEPT: Marketed as "bridging the gap between plane and helicopter", the *Sportcopter Super Sport Gyroplane* looks pretty edgy and a cool toy for those *without* acrophobia who want to avoid traffic jams. Check out the pics on the website.
COMPANY/INVENTOR: Jim Vanek, Sport Copter, Inc
FURTHER INFO: www.sportcopter.com

★ *Playboy Beach Towel (With Space For The 'Centerfold')*

CONCEPT: This cute idea from *Playboy* involves a large beach towel that looks like an enlarged *Playboy* magazine cover complete with story teasers in text except that the 'model' spot is empty and that's where the person lies, as though they are the model. See the pics at the website below for the full effect.

COMPANY/INVENTOR: Hugh Hefner's unemployed grandson?

FURTHER INFO: http://inventorspot.com/ playboy_beach_towel

★ *Magazine On A Bottle*

CONCEPT: Quite simply, this patented invention is a clever miniaturised magazine that can be attached to any consumer product, such as a bottle, to add perceived value to the original item. A classic sales promotion technique in action.

COMPANY/INVENTOR: Joanna Wojtalik, ModernMedia Concepts

FURTHER INFO: www.gizmag.com/go/4953/

★ *'SkyBlades' Rocket*

CONCEPT: The *SkyBlades is a* wind-and-release counter-spinning toy that can climb to over 100 feet.

COMPANY/INVENTOR: Via Grand Illusions

FURTHER INFO: www.grand-illusions.com/acatalog/ Skyblades.html

★ *Sonic Handgun Weapon*

CONCEPT: By emitting non-lethal ultrasonic sound, this new hand-held weapon can cause intense pain and discomfort for the target without causing any permanent harm or damage.

COMPANY/INVENTOR: Via Future Horizons

FURTHER INFO: www.futurehorizons.net/sonic.htm

★ *Key Chain Size Solar Phone Charger*
CONCEPT: This key-fob sized solar panel device can absorb energy and top-up devices like mobile phones using only solar energy. Crafty.
COMPANY/INVENTOR: Brando
FURTHER INFO: www.thegadgetblog.com/2008/03/10/brando-key-chain-size-solar-charger/

★ *Kinetic Energy Bracelet Charger*
CONCEPT: The *Kinetic Energy Bracelet Charger* stores up energy from its wearer's motion e.g. from walking or running, and can then recharge mobile devices with that clean energy.
COMPANY/INVENTOR: Wilma van Boxtel
FURTHER INFO: www.gadgettastic.com/2008/03/10/kenetic-energy-bracelet-charger/

★ *Handwarming Mouse*
CONCEPT: In colder climates, a little extra heat can be welcome and that's what appeared to have motivated this invention - a mouse that is also warm. Simple but nice.
COMPANY/INVENTOR: USB Fever
FURTHER INFO: www.geekalerts.com/usb-mouse-with-infrared-heater

★ *UV Disinfecting Scanner*
CONCEPT: Apparently capable of killing virtually 100% of germs, this hand-held UV scanner can 'disinfect' telephones, keyboards, mice, and tap knobs. Perfect for Spermatophobes and Mysophobes.
COMPANY/INVENTOR: Unknown
FURTHER INFO: www.ohgizmo.com/2008/03/04/handheld-disinfecting-uv-scanner/

★ *Rainbow Animation Flick Book*
CONCEPT: Flick books can be winners at market stalls

and this is a neat variation that recreates a rainbow by cleverly manipulating the colour spectrum and a black background.
COMPANY/INVENTOR: Masashi Kawamura
FURTHER INFO: www.utrecht.jp/person/?p=316

★ *The Orgasmo Alarm Clock*
CONCEPT: A simple concept - instead of waking up to a grating alarm, wake up to the sound of...a woman having an orgasm. There are worse sounds in the world to rise to.
COMPANY/INVENTOR: Unknown
FURTHER INFO: www.gobaz.com/prodpage.asp ?ProdID=7198

★ *Bad Milk Scanner*
CONCEPT: With a scientific explanation too geeky to contemplate (actually it senses Staphylococcus aureus in milk), this device instantly detects whether milk has gone off. Perfect for dairyphiles.
COMPANY/INVENTOR: Craig Grimes, Qingyun Cai
FURTHER INFO: www.newlaunches.com/archives/ widget_that_tells_if_your_milks_a_goner.php

★ *Easy Wake-Up Glo Pillow*
CONCEPT: As an alternative to the harsh experience of waking up to an alarm clock, the *Glo Pillow* from Ireland begins a cycle of increasing glow 40 minutes before the target wake-up time. Apparently, this is a far more soothing and 'natural' way to wake up than with a conventional alarm.
COMPANY/INVENTOR: Ian Walton, Eoin McNally
FURTHER INFO: www.ohgizmo.com/2008/03/ 13/glo-pillow-wakes-you-up-gently/

★ *Swimming Pools With Movable Floors*
CONCEPT: Thanks to this British invention, swimming

pools can either be retro-fitted or built from new with the ability to have a floor in the pool raised or lowered at the touch of a button. Such a feature allows the pool space to have multiple uses e.g. as an entertaining area during a barbeque or as a car park.

COMPANY/INVENTOR: Technology Pools
FURTHER INFO: www.technologypools.co.uk/movable_pool_floors.htm

★ *Solar-Powered Mole & Gopher Chaser*
CONCEPT: Once inserted into the ground in a garden and activated, the *Solar Mole & Gopher Chaser* intermittently emits sounds that deter moles and gophers and, perhaps, more importantly, is entirely solar powered.

COMPANY/INVENTOR: A clever mole-hater
FURTHER INFO: www.blogtoptech.info/2008/03/12/solar-mole-gopher-chaser/

★ *Artificial Venus Fly Trap*
CONCEPT: Like a real Venus Flytrap, this novel toy plant actually catches insects thanks to a motion sensor. Could be a nice impulse-buy item for kids.

COMPANY/INVENTOR: Via the Discovery Store
FURTHER INFO: www.crunchgear.com/2008/03/12/the-perfect-gift-for-the-budding-entomologist/

★ *Biometric Safe*
CONCEPT: Rather than having a safe that demands a numbered combination, this safe needs only an accepted biometric scan in order to open. It beats trying to remember a combination and offers better security than a number-based lock.

COMPANY/INVENTOR: Front Gate
FURTHER INFO: www.frontgate.com (Search on "Biometric Safe")

★ *Keyboard and Desktop Organizer (i.e. a keyboard with 'secret' storage compartment)*
CONCEPT: It is necessary to see the picture on the website below but this keyboard/ storage unit cleverly allows for the removal of desktop clutter into a computer keyboard.
COMPANY/INVENTOR: Unknown but patented
FURTHER INFO: http://nerdapproved.com/ peripherals/ps2-keyboard-and-desktop-organiser/

★ *Solar-Powered Robotic Lawn Mower*
CONCEPT: Like the hybrid lawn mower back on Page 107 of this book, the solar-powered Husqvarna, offers a green platform on which to differentiate a lawn care small business. It doesn't even require pushing as it is robotic and programmable.
COMPANY/INVENTOR: Husqvarna
FURTHER INFO: www.luxurylaunches.com/ other_stuff/husqvarnas_lawn_mower_is_solarpowered. php

★ *Color-Changing 'HotCold Mug'*
CONCEPT: Like *Hypercolor* t-shirts in the 80s which must be due for a comeback soon (http://en.wikipedia.org/wiki/Hypercolor), these heat-responsive coffee mugs change colour and embedded words appear when hot or cold. Gimmicky but fun - just like *Hypercolor* t-shirts that sold in their millions.
COMPANY/INVENTOR: Charles and Marie
FURTHER INFO: http://charlesandmarie.com

★ *Radiator Mug*
CONCEPT: The *Radiator Mug* uses the same design principle as engines and computers where 'fins' provide rapid cooling, this invention from Britain allows very hot liquid, i.e. steaming hot coffee, to be held without

discomfort by being too hot. Looks cool too.
COMPANY/INVENTOR: Stephen Reed/ Charles and Marie
FURTHER INFO: http://charlesandmarie.com

★ *Personalized Movie Poster Birthday Celebrations*
CONCEPT: As a novel gift to new parents, this customized 'movie' poster-based small business from Buffalo features the names of the parents as 'producers', other family members as 'supporting cast' and 'critic's' quotes. Cute.
COMPANY/INVENTOR: See website
FURTHER INFO: www.5starbaby.com

★ *Parent & Child Combined Day Disco*
CONCEPT: Philadelphian staged disco parties in the afternoon are now catering to parents and children bored with conventional afternoon activities and spreading to other American cities.
COMPANY/INVENTOR: Heather Murphy
FURTHER INFO: www.babylovesdisco.com

★ *Online Venue Parking Reservation*
CONCEPT: For a 15% commission, this Chicago operation offers users the ability to book car parking spaces from private sellers near major sports and entertainment venues that could only otherwise be gambled on during match day.
COMPANY/INVENTOR: ParkWhiz
FURTHER INFO: www.parkwhiz.com

★ *Mobile Paper Shredding*
CONCEPT: Companies are becoming increasingly stringent about the destruction of their records in an age where identity theft and identity fraud are skyrocketing. Mobile shredding small businesses thus offer secure

destruction of documents and environmentally conscious disposal of the waste.
COMPANY/INVENTOR: A paper-hater
FURTHER INFO: www.shredeasy.com; www.onsiteshredding.info

★ *Portable Toilet Rental*
CONCEPT: Trans/portable toilet rentals for events, sports carnivals, concerts, construction sites and public gatherings is a sound small business now as the number of public events seems to proliferate every year.
COMPANY/INVENTOR: Unknown
FURTHER INFO: www.unitedsiteservices.com; www.paradiselua.com

★ *Bullet-Proof 'Hoodies' (Streetwear)*
CONCEPT: The fact that cities feel more dangerous now as a consequence of gun and knife crime is an inescapable modern phenomenon. One British firm, using a new material called Dyneema, is thus offering *Defender* tops that can apparently stop a 9mm bullet.
COMPANY/INVENTOR: Bladerunner
FURTHER INFO: http://uk.news.yahoo.com/skynews/ 20080404/tuk-bullet-proof-hoodies-to-hit-the-stre-45dbed5.html

★ *Pedal-Powered Pub*
CONCEPT: In a clever combination of alcoholism and eco-consciousness, the *Pedalpub* from the Netherlands offers up to 16 drinkers the ability to enjoy a pint or two of beer while providing the powering of the pub by pedalling.
COMPANY/INVENTOR: Pedalpub
FURTHER INFO: www.pedalpub.com

★ *Electric Drive For Rollerblades/Skateboard*
CONCEPT: The *Easyglider X6* is an electric drive from Germany that can be attached to skateboards and rollerblades that can propel the wearer at up to 20 km/h.
COMPANY/INVENTOR: Stephan Soder
FURTHER INFO: http://easy-glider.com

★ *Self-Serve Dog Washing Vending Machine*
CONCEPT: The *K9000* is a bespoke vending machine for washing dogs. See the pictures on the website below.
COMPANY/INVENTOR: TMC Pet Vending Solutions
FURTHER INFO: www.tmcpetvending.com

★ *Transportable Hair Salon*
CONCEPT: Instead of attracting customers to a salon, this transportable, futuristic salon brings the salon to the client. See the pictures on the website below to get the full idea.
COMPANY/INVENTOR: Onsite HairCuts, HairPOD
FURTHER INFO: www.onsitehaircuts.com; www.hairpod.net

★ *Remote Control Water Sprinkler System*
CONCEPT: Given that TVs, DVDs, stereos and garage doors have had remote control functionality for a long time, applying this user-friendly principle to lawn care (also see the remote control hybrid lawn mower on Page 107) was probably inevitable.
COMPANY/INVENTOR: Unknown
FURTHER INFO: www.improvementscatalog.com/ product/id/120311.do

★ *Rumba Drum Coffee Table*
CONCEPT: When musically mute coffee tables get you down, this half-drum kit, half-coffee table could be just the thing to cheer you and your future customers up. See

the video on the website below.
COMPANY/INVENTOR: Musical Furnishings
FURTHER INFO: www.musicalfurnishings.com

★ *After Hours Beauty Salon*
CONCEPT: Through a simple and clever means of creating clear small business differentiation, a small number of New York beauty salons are now opening after hours as a means of attracting executive clientele that normally work too late to go to a normal salon. This 'after-hours' principle can be applied to many small business areas.
COMPANY/INVENTOR: Frédéric Fekkai, Red Market Salon
FURTHER INFO: www.iconoculture.com

★ *Device Recharging Vending Machine*
CONCEPT: *The Charge Box* from Britain is a powered, bespoke type of vending machine with 6 lockers wherein customers pay for a certain time increment for recharging their portable device/s. Perfect for airports.
COMPANY/INVENTOR: See below
FURTHER INFO: www.thecoolhunter.net/Gadgets/the-charge-box/

★ *LED RFID Warning LadyBag*
CONCEPT: This clever invention based on RFID technology (check out http://en.wikipedia.org/wiki/RFID if you're not sure what this is or its implications for business) flashes a warning LED light if it detects that essential items like wallet/purse and keys are not inside. A simple example of applying technology intended for one domain i.e. grocery retail, in another way.
COMPANY/INVENTOR: Team Ladybugs
FURTHER INFO: www.ladybag.official.ws; www.talk2myshirt.com/blog/archives/447

★ *Automatic Guitar Tuner*
CONCEPT: This automatic guitar tuner, possibly the first of its kind in the world, takes the 'earwork' out of guitar tuning and completes the process automatically.
COMPANY/INVENTOR: Via Action Tuners
FURTHER INFO: http://actiontuners.com

★ *Computer Programmers' Board Game*
CONCEPT: Never let it be said that nerds and geeks are incapable of having fun. This board game, *The C-jump*, is intended for children and teaches the basics of programming in Java, C and C++. While this game has limited appeal, inventing the next big new board game is an obvious path to business stardom.
COMPANY/INVENTOR: c-jump factory
FURTHER INFO: www.c-jump.com

★ *Space 'Burial' Of Ashes*
CONCEPT: If Earth is too mundane a place to store your late relative's cremated ashes, Celestis have a logical solution - send them into space!
COMPANY/INVENTOR: Celestis
FURTHER INFO: www.memorialspaceflights.com

★ *Combination Tent, Swing & Tepee - 'The Treepee'*
CONCEPT: Available as an everyday backyard play area or as a Christmas tree novelty, the *Treepee* offers a unique twist on normal tents, swings and trees used for playing. See the pics on the website below to get the drift.
COMPANY/INVENTOR: See below
FURTHER INFO: www.xmastreepee.com;
http://dvice.com/archives/2008/03/
treepee_elevate.php

★ *Virtual Coat Check*
CONCEPT: *Cloakscan* is a 21st-century system for cloak

room management that records videos of coat submission, tracks inventory and creates bar-coded tickets.
COMPANY/INVENTOR: Unknown
FURTHER INFO: www.idscan.co.uk/ uk_products_cloakscan.php

★ *Cigarette Pack Cell Phone*
CONCEPT: When talking on a cell phone, the desire to smoke at the same time is pretty strong - isn't it? This smokers-only gadget, the Wang XYW 3838, not only looks like a pack of cigarettes (a nice security feature) but can also actually carry cigarettes.
COMPANY/INVENTOR: A chain-smoking inventor from Taiwan
FURTHER INFO: http://www.trendhunter.com/ trends/the-cigarette-box-cell-phone-the-wang-xyw-3838

★ *Massaging Backpack*
CONCEPT: If you have to wear a backpack while camping or travelling the world, why not get one that massages your back as you carry it?
COMPANY/INVENTOR: Via Book of Joe
FURTHER INFO: http://www.bookofjoe.com/2008/ 03/massaging-backb.html

★ *Edible Tableware*
CONCEPT: From Japan, one eco-solution to address kitchen waste and washing up: edible tableware, *Hardtack Flatware*, is made from salt, flour and water.
COMPANY/INVENTOR: Nobuhiko Arikawa
FURTHER INFO: http://www.dezeen.com/2008/03/ 26/edible-tableware-by-rice-design/

★ *Starbucks Hot Coffee Vending Machines*
CONCEPT: In their attempt to colonize the entire

coffee-consuming world, Starbucks have now introduced their own branded hot coffee vending machines as a way to reach places where their ever-growing branch of stores cannot.

COMPANY/INVENTOR: Starbucks
FURTHER INFO: www.adcult.com/ads/starbucks-introduces-hot-drink-machines/

★ *Compostable Potato Cutlery*
CONCEPT: Instead of adding to the world's congested trash mountains, one small measure that could help and prove an intriguing small business proposition is this potato-based cutlery (20% soy oil, 80% potato starch), *Spudware*, that can be composted and is biodegrade.
COMPANY/INVENTOR: Via Spluch
FURTHER INFO: http://spluch.blogspot.com/2007/10/cutlery-made-from-potatoes.html

★ *$100 Cups Of Cat-Poo Coffee*
CONCEPT: By mixing the extremely rare Kopi Luwak bean freshly 'expelled' from a rare Indonesian cat through its faeces into coffee, one London entrepreneur has created an exotic new coffee brew in London that sells for £50/$100 a cup. Would Ripley believe this?
COMPANY/INVENTOR: Peter Jones Via Spluch
FURTHER INFO: www.mirror.co.uk/news/topstories/2008/04/10/cat-poo-50-a-cup-89520-20378143/

~

~

13.
Shop/Stall/Retail:
The Latest & Greatest
Small Business Ideas That Need
A Shop/Store/Retail/Location
Presence.

~

SMALL BUSINESS ENTRY LEGEND

Please read this Legend for a full understanding of the Small Business Idea entries below. Also note that most of the small businesses below have attempted to add an element of novelty and thus competitive advantage to an existing product or service.

Such a principle is a proven method for small business success.

Don't forget, there is not any form of in-depth analysis in *400 Latest & Greatest Small Business Ideas* as many other books focus on specific small businesses e.g. running a vending machine business (an excellent type of starting small business, by the way and many innovations in that area are briefly covered in this book).

The intention here is to give you a massively *broad* - but not deep - 'snapshot' of small business innovation in the world today. When you find a business or small businesses that appeals, fully deconstructing the business model of the web examples of these businesses in the entry here is your first logical starting point. You should then purchase other reference works that go into that type of business in much more detail.

As discussed above, many of the 400+ business concepts discussed throughout this book, including the above 'X-File' Small Businesses presented, work on THREE vital principles:

1. Most, but not all, have a very low potential financial downside. Small businesses that require huge amounts of capital to start up are far too risky given the statistics of small business failures. If most of the 400+ businesses below failed (for whatever reason), it would NOT be financially catastrophic

for the stakeholders. Absorbing the best microcosmic tactical advice on small business on Page 267 is also *highly* recommended.

2. Apart from the classic, blue-chip small businesses that are always worth considering, some of which we felt needed to be included here, most of the 'real world' small businesses listed here usually possess a degree of differentiation from existing businesses - typically one or more angles that give significant marketing leverage over competitors. This is not a book listing the same old small business clichés but rather a comprehensive survey of innovative, lateral-thinking-driven, 21st century small businesses.

3. Potential problems or caveats are highlighted in order that any small business entrepreneur wishing to pursue a certain concept is aware and thus prepared to work around such inherent difficulties - which all businesses have in some form and have to be solved; problem-solving being an indispensable skill for the small business entrepreneur. However, the websites of actual small business for that entry prove that such hurdles were overcome by others so why not you?

★ *Indicates the type of small business recommended.*
CONCEPT: Explains the concept in more detail.
STRENGTHS: Why this business is a potential winner. A phrase I often feature - "senior-friendly small business" - indicates that this business could be suitable for a senior/retired person; a great way to fight back against our society's scandalous age-discrimination. Though most small businesses here could be successfully operated by a senior, I have only highlighted the very easiest of these with the above description.
WEAKNESSES: Any caveats to watch out for and thus reduce or eliminate in execution.
REAL WORLD BIZ: Web address/es of actual businesses of this type in the 'real world' from which you can observe their marketing, pricing and any other relevant details.

For example:

★ *Umbrella Vending Machines*

CONCEPT: In rainy cities, vending machines selling cheap umbrellas are strategically placed to maximise the need for protection from the rain.

STRENGTHS: If located in busy subway/train stations, shopping or business areas, sales should be outstanding; the owner does not need to be present to operate business; unique form of vending machine; no competition; senior-friendly small business.

WEAKNESSES: Dependent on rainy weather; the need to secure strategic locations for maximum sales; specialised nature of machines in terms of servicing.

REAL WORLD BIZ: www.umbrollys.com; www.umbrellabox.sg

~

★ *Pizza-In-A-Cone*

CONCEPT: Unsatisfied with giving us great works of art like the Alfa Romeo GTV6, those stylish Italians have topped themselves with this killer pizza new variation: *Pizza-In-A-Cone*. Check the website for all the details.

STRENGTHS: Unique; fun; ground floor opportunity; massive potential customer base; can you imagine how popular this would be at a busy market?

WEAKNESSES: Not many but a retail location is mandatory and that opens the usual issues of site rental, staffing and overheads.

REAL WORLD BIZ: www.konopizza.com

★ *Indoor Skydiving Center*

CONCEPT: As a leisure alternative, a specialised room with a massive fan built into the floor recreates most of the sensations of skydiving as users 'fly' horizontally above the floor - without the threat of parachute failure.

STRENGTHS: Different form of entertainment; very rare business so far; additional income available from offering souvenir photos or videos of users' flying experience; relatively easy to set up.

WEAKNESSES: Some capital expenditure required; staff needed; certain health and safety regulations would be applicable.

REAL WORLD BIZ: www.airkix.com; www.iflyhollywood.com; www.skyventurecolorado.com; www.skydiveperris.com/tunnel.html

★ *ATM Franchisee/Operator*

CONCEPT/ANGLE: ATMs in some local stores are operated by an entrepreneurial franchisee who receives a fee for each transaction. A variation on this business is that the entrepreneur operates the ATM/s as a standalone business *without* a franchise and through their own commercial relationships with banks et al.

STRENGTHS: Very little physical work required once established (basically it's a cash vending machine).
WEAKNESSES: Harder to find locations without ATMs; need to negotiate for ATM 'real estate' (e.g. in a local store); (relatively) high start-up costs; cash handling security.
REAL WORLD BIZ: www.acfnfranchise.com; www.mandrakeatm.com; www.astracomm.co.uk; www.omnicash.biz

★ *Exploitation Free/Sustainable Products Store*
CONCEPT: In an age where consumers are becoming increasingly concerned about the environmental and ethical impact of their shopping, a shop that solely stocks 'exploitation-free' products offers consumers with a social conscience such an alternative - how about '*Humane*'?
STRENGTHS: Suits one of the dominant trends emerging among consumers today; positive contribution to society; nature of store would attract a great deal of free media coverage.
WEAKNESSES: Capital expenditure; need to occupy conventional retail site *or* market stall location at first before expanding; inventory ties up money; problems associated with sourcing products such as clothing items that are *not* sourced from sweatshops and guaranteeing their practices; possibly some own small-scale self-manufacturing required.
REAL WORLD BIZ: www.care2.com/shopping/; www.wildorganics.net; www.nigelsecostore.com; www.animalaidshop.org.uk; www.api4animals.org/store_index.php

★ *Indoor Bungee Jumping*
CONCEPT: In an effort to maximize the bungee jumping experience, The UK Bungee Club in Sheffield have adapted bungee jumping for indoor exhilaration (150 feet

fall), complete with giant video screens, loud music and spotlights swirling through semi-darkness. Obviously normal bungee jumping was too placid for these extreme entrepreneurial lunatics.

STRENGTHS: Unique; word-of-mouth potential; fun; should attract customers from a large catchment area; spinoff businesses in the same venue e.g. classes, apparel; cafes (sub-let to help with overheads?).

WEAKNESSES: Venue set-up costs; staffing; safety regulation adherence; fluctuation of custom during the week.

REAL WORLD BIZ: www.ukbungee.co.uk/ the_abyss_at_magna.html

★ *Video Surfing Simulator*

CONCEPT: Video Surf Nut have created a surfing video simulation machine where customers can stand on a full size surfboard and 'surf' on a big 'wave' on a large video screen next to them. It's an interesting novelty and works well at fairs, malls and public gatherings.

STRENGTHS: Machine is relatively simple as it is based on a PS2 and only weighs 35 pounds; vendor can either rent or site the surf simulator; fun; different; should arouse consumer curiosity; fast set-up.

WEAKNESSES: Nothing significant compared with other types of small business – this has excellent potential.

REAL WORLD BIZ: www.videosurfnut.com

★ *Inflatable Amusements at Markets, Fairs, Parties*

CONCEPT: Inflatable amusements are sited in fairs, schools, markets, or outdoor events for children to play on for a set price/time limit. Inflatables aren't limited just to bouncy castles, there is a big range of very cool new slippery slide-based bouncies, mazes, water slide bouncies, game-based bouncies, 'moonwalk' bouncies and others now – see the phenomenal ranges on the websites below. One interesting possible variation would be to gain permission to set up in a large supermarket car park and combine child care with the bouncy attraction so that parents could shop by themselves while their children are entertained.

STRENGTHS: The 'pester power' of children; fun; no shortage of business in the right location; brilliant new inflatable variations coming out all the time; expandability.

WEAKNESSES: Cost of purchase of inflatables; potential damage to inflatables from children; delivery and removal requires suitable vehicle.

REAL WORLD BIZ: www.gazinflatables.co.uk; www.jumbo.co.uk; www.bounce-a-lot.co.uk; www.inflationcreations.net

★ *Rodeo Bull-Riding Machine*

CONCEPT: If people are bored with arcade 'shoot-em-ups', trying to ride a rampaging mechanical rodeo 'bull' could be the answer. The machine/s can be hired out for parties, corporate events or fairs *or* set up as a coin-pay ride in a public location.

STRENGTHS: Novel; challenging; fun.

WEAKNESSES: Possible injury to riders; cost of the bull and its maintenance, what if it stampedes?

REAL WORLD BIZ: www.djphantom.com/ mechanicalbull.htm; www.rodeoleisure.co.uk; www.bigfun.com.au; www.mechanicalbull.com.au

★ *Private Mailbox Center*

CONCEPT: Government post offices with mailboxes usually have none available and hold a long waiting list for vacancies. Open an accessible room/area with private mailboxes.

STRENGTHS: Very little work required after set-up;

like a vending machine business, business can work without owner's attendance.

WEAKNESSES: Finding/renting suitable premises; initial marketing blitz to attract clients; ceiling on possible income dependent on number of mailboxes - though you could open other mailbox centres in nearby areas.

REAL WORLD BIZ: www.americanpostbox.com; www.pakmail.com/services/private.asp; www.mailboxesunlimited.com

★ *Adopt-An-Olive Tree/Wine Vine*

CONCEPT: Nudo, an Italian business, offers olive trees for annual 'adoption' in return for all of the produce from the 'adopted' tree during that year. Similarly, other small vineyards are starting to offer 'rental' or 'adoption' of specific vines in their vineyards as a means of securing annual business revenue. Such small business ventures can also fund a dramatic lifestyle change and financially support a cool 'life in the country.'

STRENGTHS: Great lifestyle in the country; 'adoption' secures income against weather/climate disasters as annual fee is paid regardless; suits wine lovers well.

WEAKNESSES: Potential revenue is always limited by the number of trees or vines available; as more small businesses use this approach, attracting clients could become harder though this form of business could be used to supplement rather than replace income; cost of the farm or land in the first place and set-up expenses.

REAL WORLD BIZ: www.nudo-italia.com; www.sthelenawinery.com/adopt.html; www.wineshare.co.uk

★ *Cappuccino Artist*

CONCEPT: Adding a twist to a conventional coffee service in a public location, some small business owners with a little creative flair are using the tops of their customers' coffee to create a brief and often brilliant artwork. This novelty is particularly popular and generates excellent word-of-mouth curiosity.

STRENGTHS: Original; fun; difficult for a Starbucks, Costa or Caffe Nero to replicate.

WEAKNESSES: Requires some creative flair or willingness to learn basics of 'cappuccino art' (see websites below); normal coffee business set-up expenses still apply.

REAL WORLD BIZ: www.latteart.org/latteart.htm; www.vancouvercoffee.ca/archives/2006/11/sammy-lin-coffee-art.html; http://haha.nu/beautiful/howto-make-cappuccino-art/

★ *Zubbles Colored Bubbles*

CONCEPT: Created by Ascadia, *Zubbles* are richly coloured bubbles that can be sold from a market stall, at fairs or in malls.

STRENGTHS: Unique; fun; businesses that harness the 'pester power' of children to persuade their parents to buy something usually do extremely well; only a small real estate footprint is needed in a busy location.

WEAKNESSES: Cannot be operated from home so some space rental is needed though market stall prices are usually reasonable.

REAL WORLD BIZ: www.zubbles.com

★ *Colonic Hydrotherapy*

CONCEPT: Colonic hydrotherapy or 'colonic irrigation', an alternative health care treatment, is used to maintain the colon in good health. A full explanation of the therapy can be found at www.colonic-association.org/hydrotherapy.html. This therapy has particular appeal among our older citizens (and our population *is* aging rapidly) and once tried, its apparent health benefits create strong repeat business.

STRENGTHS: Very little competition – if any; gratitude of patients who gain a greater sense of wellbeing from treatments; strong repeat business and word-of-mouth once established; potential to expand into multiple locations is strong; regular treatments can reduce risk of colon cancer.

WEAKNESSES: Need to publicise the health benefits of the treatment if unknown in your area; people are reluctant to try treatment at first as it can be perceived as invasive – some free/discount trialling may be necessary; suits business operators comfortable with working intimately with the human body; initial equipment set-up costs and public location.

REAL WORLD BIZ: www.thevinecentre.com; www.colonicwellbeing.co.uk; www.aqualibria.com; www.colonic-association.org

★ *Solar-powered Vending Machines*

CONCEPT: Solar Energy Vending, a Spanish vending machine innovator, has developed a standalone solar-powered vending machine that can be positioned outdoors – free from the needs of a power cord - in high traffic areas such as beaches, ski fields, parks and golf courses. Machines are available now from Solar Energy Vending.

STRENGTHS: These specialised machines have options of wind turbine substitute for solar cells if sunlight is poor; generous tax advantages for renewable energy in some territories; novelty factor should generate positive free media attention; normal benefits of operating a vending machine business – mainly, machine/s earn income while owner is absent.

WEAKNESSES: Vulnerability of machine/s to vandalism away from buildings; higher purchase cost of machines; like any vending machine business, success hinges on the ability to negotiate great high-traffic sites for the machines.

REAL WORLD BIZ: www.solarvending.com

★ *Mobile Phone Vending Machine*

CONCEPT: Vodafone in the UK have trialled mobile phone vending machines partly targeted at travellers seeking a quick second phone for a travelling companion or themselves – usually on a prepaid basis. As such, these types of machines will inevitably become available for smart vending machine operators to snap up and site for themselves.

STRENGTHS: All of the typical advantages of vending machines with a unique product offered; much higher per-unit profit than normal vending machine products.

WEAKNESSES: Greater need for security given the desirability of inventory for thieves; more specialised servicing requirements; higher inventory cost than normal vending machine products.

REAL WORLD BIZ: www.business-idea.com/ShowPosting.asp?ID=1991; www.americasnetwork.com/americasnetwork/article/articleDetail.jsp?id=374294; www.informationweek.com/hardware/showArticle.jhtml?articleID=202803459

★ *Bicycle Vending Machine*

CONCEPT: In the Netherlands, BikeDispenser.com has successfully introduced an urban bicycle-rental stand which is organised to work in the manner of a U-Haul with one-way trips on RFID-chip equipped bikes to other stands throughout the city.

STRENGTHS: Great way to combat urban air pollution and therefore – in theory – should be supported by governments of all levels; suits surging tide of green consumerism across the Western world; unique service.

WEAKNESSES: Need for theft-prevention

mechanisms; government support essential in licensing and facilitation; setup costs; finding of locations to create necessary network.

REAL WORLD BIZ: www.bikedispenser.com

★ *Pizza Vending Machine*

CONCEPT: After considerable Research & Development, Wonderpizza, have released a pizza vending machine capable of producing oven-baked pizzas in two minutes. These machines are now available from Wonderpizza to small business operators all over the world.

STRENGTHS: Unique; novelty aspect of the machine will arouse consumer curiosity; potential for outstanding returns to early adopters establishing footholds in strategic high-traffic locations; higher per-unit profit than conventional vending machine products.

WEAKNESSES: Restocking of ingredients in machine/s more frequent than conventional vending machines; strategic location placement just as fundamental as any other vending machine operation.

REAL WORLD BIZ: http://wonderpizzausa.com

★ *Flowboard/Freebords Skateboards*

CONCEPT: *Flowboards* and *Freeboards* are large skateboards that mimic the behaviour of snowboards. If they aren't available in your area yet, a definite opportunity exists to cash in on this new trend.

STRENGTHS: New; unique; fun; profitable.

WEAKNESSES: May require a retail presence (though eBay is an obvious but more competitive option); cost of inventory; business probably only suits certain types of small business owners.

REAL WORLD BIZ: www.freebordssouthwest.co.uk; www.freebord.co.uk; www.flowsport.co.uk; www.flowlab.com

★ *15 Minute Pizza Delivery*

CONCEPT: Wisconsin's Super Fast Pizza has pioneered 15-minute pizza delivery by using specialized vans capable of cooking pizzas while moving. Through wi-fi, the mobile vans simultaneously take orders, cook and make deliveries. If there isn't one of these in your area yet, you could be the first.

STRENGTHS: Speed of delivery will attract consumers; novelty value should generate free media coverage; *very* frequent repeat business if properly run.

WEAKNESSES: Cost of vans; normal staffing issues.

REAL WORLD BIZ: www.msnbc.msn.com/id/ 7726695/

★ *Bikini/Bodybuilder Carwash Events & Promotions*

CONCEPT: This small business is pretty old though the businesses below have taken it to another level by offering bikini car washes as corporate events and other promotional activities. They even sell DVDs of their car-washing girls in action.

STRENGTHS: Sex appeal sells; low equipment costs; staff employed on a 'per car' or 'per event' basis; working with pretty girls/guys.

WEAKNESSES: Needs a warmish climate; may not suit everyone's morality; staffing issues like every other business though added difficulty of physical appeal criterion; if run solely as a car wash, location/s is critical.

REAL WORLD BIZ: www.detroitbikinicarwash.com; www.kwicherbichen.com/car-washes.htm

★ *Bonsai Dealer*

CONCEPT: Interest in Japanese bonsai plants is high at the moment and certain types of exotic bonsai sell for thousands of dollars. Being a dealer in bonsai, either online or in the real world (some bonsai entrepreneurs set up *within* larger garden centres) constitutes a potentially lucrative business, depending on existing competition in your area. Classes in bonsai care can also be added as a second income stream.

STRENGTHS: Working with nature; artistic fulfilment.
WEAKNESSES: Competition in your area already (though it could be poorly done); time that bonsai take to grow before sale; space needed for them to grow.
REAL WORLD BIZ: www.bonsaiboy.com; www.wsbonsai.com; www.bonsaidirect.co.uk; www.bonsaitrees.com; www.plantcitybonsai.com

★ Tea Room

CONCEPT: Think of a coffee joint like Nero or Starbucks, except that a Tea Room specializes in tea. It's a quaint, classy alternative to coffee but is expensive to set up. Another alternative is to become an online exotic tea dealer through eBay for a fraction of the cost – even as a stepping stone to your own Tea Room.
STRENGTHS: Tea is popular and has a certain *olde worlde* charm; customer fatigue with McStarbucks-style coffee venues; word-of-mouth potential for 'fad' activity.
WEAKNESSES: High start-up costs; staffing; ongoing overheads.
REAL WORLD BIZ: www.thetearoom.com.au; http://greattearoomsofamerica.com; www.camelliatearoom.com; www.savannahtearoom.com

★ Ice Cream 'Hot Dogs'

CONCEPT: As a market day and killer fast food variation, ice cream packaged and presented like a hot dog has obvious impulse buying appeal - especially with children.
STRENGTHS: Fun; novel; impulse buy-oriented; easy to set up.
WEAKNESSES: Retail location necessary; keeping up with demand from hungry children?

REAL WORLD BIZ: www.cooldoginc.com

★ *Film/Video/Tape/Data Storage*
CONCEPT: Every year, more and more film-makers and digital videographers make projects as vehicles for film business success. These individuals need a suitable place to store their raw footage under the right conditions. Films tend to shoot anything from four to fifty times the amount of material that winds up in the final program. Yet the original material is usually always kept for 'making of' and 'special features' options later.
STRENGTHS: Apart from the facility (which could be unmanned), there is very little ongoing maintenance required for the ongoing charge to clients.
WEAKNESSES: Facility needs space; security and right atmospheric conditions needed for best preservation of film and video stock; fairly high start-up cost though business could be expanded in stages.
REAL WORLD BIZ: www.preferredmedia.com.au; www.undergroundvaults.com/offerings/itemsstored/mo viefilmstorage.cfm; www.hollywoodvaults.com; www.filmcore.net/html/2000/vaultinginformation.html;

★ *Self-Storage Management*
CONCEPT: As all of our lives are becoming more cluttered with 'stuff' that we don't seem willing to throw away, the storage rental industry is booming. This is a blue-chip small business that is easy to finance, easy to run and easy to profit from.
STRENGTHS: Low effort required for rental charge once facility's self-storage units are rented; booming industry; rental rates can be indexed each year with existing customers who don't want to move their gear.
WEAKNESSES: Start-up cost; need for suitable premises and capital or franchise from existing chain.
REAL WORLD BIZ: www.kss.com.au/new/;

www.safestore.co.uk; www.extraspace.com; www.ustoreit.com; www.usaselfstorage.com

★ *Laundromat & Internet Café*

CONCEPT: Individually, the Laundromat and Internet Café (which is *still* an excellent small business, by the way) have been around for a long time. As they potentially both appeal to a similar market, a natural synergy exists where the two are combined – as the businesses below illustrate.

STRENGTHS: Unique; allows a business to develop multiple revenue streams from one location e.g. washing, drying, washing powder, net surfing, printing.

WEAKNESSES: Set-up costs are high, especially on the Laundromat side; would require staff presence to maintain security of IT equipment (unlike a 'set-and-forget' Laundromat); need to make sure that the visual 'vibe' of the place reflects an Internet Café more than an 'old-school' Laundromat.

REAL WORLD BIZ: www.cyclonelaundry.com; www.halfbakery.com/idea/laundrynet

★ *Parasailing*

CONCEPT: Parasailing, where a boat tows a person strapped into a parachute and they go up and down as the boat accelerates or decelerates, is great fun. It can also be a very lucrative business if set up in the right leisure area.

STRENGTHS: Big returns on busy days; outdoor lifestyle; businesses that create fun are more enjoyable than more practical ones.

WEAKNESSES: High start-up costs inc. boats which can exceed $50,000; need to find suitable location; rigorous adherence to safety laws and regulations required.

REAL WORLD BIZ: www.daytonaparasailing.com; www.parasailcity.com; www.parasailingcatalina.com;

www.parasail-nz.co.nz

★ *'Bed and Breakfast' Specializing in Gay/Disabled/Senior/Family Market*
CONCEPT: Conventional B & Bs are fantastic businesses in a suitable house in a suitable location – especially given the increasing travel mobility of the world's population. Passenger air travel volume, for example, is expected to double in the next thirty years. So if your house is in a desirable area for tourists/travellers and there is already an abundance of B & Bs, why not specialize in the booming gay or disabled travel sectors? One trick for B & B operators is to situate their operation adjacent to extremely popular tourist areas e.g. setting up in Squamish for Whistler-bound travellers. However, by differentiating a B & B, such as through the above variations, even more business can be attracted. Many good books now exist on successfully operating a B & B so check with those if this small business model sounds appealing.
STRENGTHS: Houses can be relatively easily adapted to demands of B & B use, even for disabled use; the fact that your house is the site of business saves an enormous amount of money on set-up costs; social interaction with guests; once established, the business could be sold at a considerable profit.
WEAKNESSES: May be the need for certain licences to operate as a B & B in your area; income can be seasonal.
REAL WORLD BIZ: www.disabled-holidays-wales.co.uk (Disabled); www.pinkuk.com/Tourism/b_b.asp (Gay); http://gay9.com/bandb/index.php3?category=2 (Gay); www.coachhousecrookham.com (Disabled)

★ *Women Only Backpackers' Hostel*
CONCEPT: Dormitory and single-room backpackers'

hostels have long proven to be excellent small businesses. Taking that already-successful model a step further by adding differentiation, some hostels around the world are now targeting women travelling together and offering the perceived/actual extra security of being 'women only'.

STRENGTHS: Unique appeal; listings in *Lonely Planet* and *Let's Go* type guides should ensure solid bookings throughout the year; internet booking options; social interaction with travellers; feelgood factor in providing an appreciated service.

WEAKNESSES: Must be run by women; seasonal income like normal hostels; high set-up cost if hostel venue is rented or purchased.

REAL WORLD BIZ: www.jacobycottage.co.uk; www.bnb.it/beb/; www.divaespana.com www.thebutterflyinn.com/aloha.html

★ *(Mobile?) Alternative Therapist e.g. Aromatherapy/ Reflexology/Rolfing/ Osteomyology/Kinesiology*

CONCEPT: Alternative therapies are continually gaining in popularity as disenchantment with the traditional medical establishment grows. Services offered from a central location, or, even better, in clients' homes thus capitalize on this trend.

STRENGTHS: Perceived value of therapeutic services is high with many practitioners charging $100+ an hour; highly portable business, can be practised anywhere in the world; repeat business potential is strong.

WEAKNESSES: Most therapeutic qualifications require study from 1-3 years; office set-up costs (unless working from home on a mobile basis, which makes far more economic sense, especially during the early stages of the operation).

REAL WORLD BIZ: www.rolfing.org; www.aromatherapy.com; www.alternative-therapies.com; www.homeopathyhome.com;

www.homeopathic.org; www.kinesiologyfederation.org; www.osteomyology.co.uk

★ *Portuguese Chicken Burger Outlet*
CONCEPT: In Australia, a wave of Portuguese chicken burger outlets have quickly threatened the dominance of the fast food franchises (especially www.oporto.com.au). If you are in a country or area where this fad has not taken off, consider it.
STRENGTHS: High franchisability; proven formula for success; impulse-buy-oriented.
WEAKNESSES: Usual set-up costs associated with a fast food retail location: overheads, staffing, finding a venue with sufficient human traffic.
REAL WORLD BIZ: www.oporto.com.au

★ *Specialist Immigration Consultant*
CONCEPT: In our multicultural world, global migration is now massive. And, as a consequence, those individuals migrating from one specific country to another e.g Bulgaria to Britain or Mexico to US, need *specific* consulting advice for their *specific* migration. That situation thus demands small businesses focused on their *specific* migration needs.
STRENGTHS: Word-of-mouth marketing potential within specific ethnic community; the opportunity to dominate one niche market segment; social relationships; repeat business through other family members' or friends' migration.
WEAKNESSES: Demands thorough knowledge of immigration process and comfort dealing with government institutions; some licensing may be required; overheads; time needed to build the business.
REAL WORLD BIZ: www.canreach.com; www.migrationbureau.com

★ *Self-Defence Coaching by Women for Women*

CONCEPT: Like women who set up small businesses to appeal to a mainly female clientele as a result of the frustrating attitudes of some men in business, personal self-defence coaching by a woman for another woman is an emerging sub-niche. This small business could be a great adjunct to a women's-only gym, another popular small business spinoff in today's health and fitness industry.

STRENGTHS: Rewarding work; relationships with clients; word-of-mouth marketing potential; no product inventory as it is a service and knowledge-based small business; can have a home-based spinoff where the instructor travels to clients' homes.

WEAKNESSES: Time taken to acquire self-defence skills - Jiu-jitsu and Kyokushinkai Karate are highly recommended; venue hire cost though only on a per class basis.

REAL WORLD BIZ: www.safetyforwomen.com

★ *Exotic Diorama Sales at Markets*

CONCEPT: With today's technology, constructing breathtaking dioramas is relatively easy for anyone with creative flair. A diorama is a microsomic world in a box, like a miniature stage, fully dressed with a particular theme e.g. a Civil War battle, a doll's house, dinosaur battle or even a biblical 'freeze-frame' – it's entirely up to the creator. Like other slightly unusual 'gimmicks' (think lava lamps), items like visually striking dioramas do well at markets and fairs, especially those targeted at children. An online spinoff is an obvious extension of the business.

STRENGTHS: Visually impressive; provokes impulse-buy; great for children; enjoyable craft; imaginative.

WEAKNESSES: How many can be made and sold in a day/week/month?; requires some artistic flair.

REAL WORLD BIZ: www.ehow.com/

how_12761_make-diorama.html;
http://photos.si.edu/dino/cretac.gif

★ *Kitesurfing/Kiteboarding Sales/Classes*

CONCEPT: Kitesurfing, also known as kiteboarding, is emerging as a popular water sport, albeit an extreme one. Being the only/best/cheapest seller of kiteboards and associated apparel and accessories in your area could prove to be a profitable small business.

STRENGTHS: Edgy; extreme; different; appeals to younger impulse-driven buyers; spinoff business potential e.g. classes, apparel.

WEAKNESSES: Usual retail issues of location (unless run as online business initially), staffing and overheads; needs to be situated near water; how long will the fad last?

REAL WORLD BIZ: www.kitesurfing.ie; www.flyingfishonline.com; www.kitesurfuk.com; www.bestkiteboarding.com.

★ *Halal Food Specialist*

CONCEPT: Is your local Muslim community properly catered for in terms of Halal foods? This ideally suits someone of Islamic background but dominance of such a niche is a definite possibility with this small business.

STRENGTHS: Niche; sector domination; spinoff businesses targeted at Muslim community.

WEAKNESSES: Needs a great site; inventory costs; set-up costs; usual staffing and overhead issues; possibility of established competitors.

REAL WORLD BIZ: www.zabihah.com (searchable listings across US)

★ *'School of Rock' Owner*

CONCEPT: Imagine a music school that focuses on *only* on rock music - much like Jack Black's character did at the end of *School of Rock*. Franchises like that of RockMasters below are also available.

STRENGTHS: Fun; popularity of rock music; cooler than conventional business; expandable.

WEAKNESSES: Centre overheads; finding and keeping good rock-god, music teachers.

REAL WORLD BIZ: www.rockmasters.net

★ *Modular Backyard Garden Offices*

CONCEPT: Garden Lodges, a British company, specializes in purpose-built garden offices. Planning permission is usually not required for installation.

STRENGTHS: Offers a great escape from the proverbial 'Rat Race'; visually pleasing; different; targets home-based small businesses well.

WEAKNESSES: Display centre cost; inventory cost; low repeat business cycle; staffing.

REAL WORLD BIZ: www.gardenlodges.co.uk

★ *Bridge Climb/Walk Travel Experiences*

CONCEPT: Now rated as one of the best tourist attractions in Australia, the small business entrepreneurs behind the now iconic Sydney Harbour Bridge Walk spent years convincing the relevant authorities of the merit and safety of their venture - tethered walkers making their way along maintenance access paths to the top of the Harbour Bridge, over 130 meters above the harbour. This small business has been phenomenally successful, profitable and is often booked out months ahead. Any similarly spectacular bridges near you for a copycat venture?

STRENGTHS: Unique = higher charges; spectacular experiences offered; word-of-mouth marketing; office can be home-based and customers met at the bridge, hence lowering overheads.

WEAKNESSES: Getting approval and affordable

insurance; possibly seasonal; only suits entrepreneurs who are not terrified by heights.

REAL WORLD BIZ: www.bridgeclimb.com

★ *Wind Turbines for Homes*

CONCEPT: Electricity-generating micro wind turbines have never been smaller, cheaper or easier to install than they are today. Undoubtedly they will become even more so in the future. Given the rise of eco-consumerism, selling these green energy creators looks like the basis of an excellent small business. A little known fact is that homes are actually much bigger polluters of our environment than cars.

STRENGTHS: Eco-consciousness friendly; relatively cheap; easy to fit; feelgood factor.

WEAKNESSES: Competitors; need for showroom; constantly developing technologies that need to be followed.

REAL WORLD BIZ: www.wirefreedirect.com/wind_turbines.asp; www.energyenv.co.uk/D400WindTurbine.asp; www.alternative-energy.co.uk; www.reuk.co.uk/D400-Wind-Generator.htm

★ *Green Walls/Vertical Gardens for Offices*

CONCEPT: Corporations and companies have long been accustomed to hiring plants to beautify their offices. However, the latest fashion in this small business realm is the hiring of 'green walls', 'vertical gardens' or 'plantwalls' which are striking artistic additions to any company foyer. See the pics on the websites below.

STRENGTHS: Novel; interesting; visually impressive; can benefit from 'me-too' fad factor.

WEAKNESSES: Same as a conventional plant hire business i.e. need for space to grow and maintain plants, suitable vehicle and acquisition of clients through advertising, marketing and cold calling.

REAL WORLD BIZ: www.greenfortune.com, www.indoorlandscaping.de

★ *Gay Mens Wedding Attire*
CONCEPT: This is a specialist retail store in Spain focused on wedding suits and fashion for *gay* weddings.
STRENGTHS: Unique; would attract free media attention; we are living in the *Queer Eye* age.
WEAKNESSES: Usual factors affecting store locations such as leasing/rental costs, staffing, utilities; smaller market (but a large share of that smaller market).
REAL WORLD BIZ: www.bybcn.es/english.htm

★ *Amphibious Bus-Boat Trolleyboats*
CONCEPT: Trolleyboats are large, open, tourism-friendly buses that also happen to be boats capable of water travel. For small business operators living near water, this could be well worth investigating. Check out the pics on the website below to get the picture.
STRENGTHS: Could be unique in your area; fun; impressive returns when busy; trolley boat is an excellent billboard for itself.
WEAKNESSES: Cost of purchase/lease of trolleyboat; seasonal nature of tourism; maintenance costs.
REAL WORLD BIZ: www.trolleyboats.com

★ *Indoor/Outdoor Miniature Car Racing Track*
CONCEPT: Micro Reality has created a stunning miniature motor racing track that can be situated indoors or outdoors. Little boys of all ages will love playing 'boy racer' on this impressive set-up.
STRENGTHS: Visually impressive; suits lovers of cars well; fun; unique; arguably more engaging than simple video driving machines – these are real miniature cars on a real miniature track.
WEAKNESSES: Needs considerable set-up space;

initial cost of equipment (though recoverable quickly if sited properly).
REAL WORLD BIZ: www.microreality.com

★ *Microsoft Certified IT Course & Qualification Provider*
CONCEPT: Individuals and companies are constantly looking to upgrade their IT qualifications and knowledge base. Depending on the IT Qualification Providers in your area - or not - there may be an opportunity to set up such a small business. While this isn't a small business that is fast to set up, all businesses, large and small are only going to get more IT-focused, not less, in the foreseeable future.
STRENGTHS: Repeat business from big corporations; courses are charged at high prices; IT nature of virtually all business now; strong demand for IT courses.
WEAKNESSES: Possibly best suited to someone with IT/IT education or IT management background; substantial set-up before returns; overheads, though venues could be hired on a per-course basis; ongoing knowledge development required as new programs come out; possibly competitors already established in your target area but it is a massive market.
REAL WORLD BIZ: www.nhnj.com; www.setfocus.com; www.computeach.co.uk; www.career-in-it.co.uk; www.firebrandtraining.co.uk

★ *Back Rubber Vending Machine Chair*
CONCEPT: Among vending machine variations - arguably just about the best form of small business for a first-time entrepreneur - this one appeals nicely to impulse-spending, sensual satisfaction: an automated back rubbing chair 'massage.'
STRENGTHS: Low start-up cost; earns income while operator absent.
WEAKNESSES: Success heavily reliant on suitable

high-traffic location; cost of chair and maintenance.
REAL WORLD BIZ: www.thebackrubber.com

★ *Problem Pet Troubleshooter*
CONCEPT: TV programs like *It's Me Or The Dog* on
Britain's Channel 4 (www.channel4.com/entertainment/
tv/microsites/I/itsmeorthedog/index.html) illustrate that
many pet owners lack the skills to care properly for their
animals. To this end, a dog-loving individual can build a
successful small business based on curing dogs of their
anti-social behaviours.
STRENGTHS: Working with animals; satisfaction of
'curing' pet and owner alike; project-oriented small
business; no inventory, just all knowledge and skill - with
animals *and* people; very low overheads.
WEAKNESSES: Working with disturbed animals; low
repeat business cycle; human owners usually need much
more training than the animals; intensive study probably
required.
REAL WORLD BIZ: www.furrylittlemonsters.co.uk;
www.talkingtodogs.com; www.ehow.com/
how_2073629_become-pet-psychologist.html

★ *Naturist Venue Operator*
CONCEPT: Naturism or nudism is a popular niche
pastime and venues across the world do well catering
exclusively to this niche. If you find clothes annoying, this
could be your first/next small business venture.
STRENGTHS: Freedom from clothes!; not many
competitors; save money on staff uniforms; easy to tap
into naturism market through naturism websites,
internet forums and focused magazines; repeat business
potential.
WEAKNESSES: Venue cost; gymnophobia.
REAL WORLD BIZ: www.aanr.com;
www.euronat.fr/en/index.asp; www.lupinlodge.org;

www.calienteresorts.com

★ *Jet Ski Hire*

CONCEPT: Is there a popular body of water near you that does *not* have a jet ski rental small business? Take a drive and check it out. It could be a great business opportunity for you - at least for the warmer months of the year.

STRENGTHS: Outdoors; fun; your business presence at the beach/river/lake may be all the advertising you need - especially with a giant banner there saying: "Jet ski $60 for 30 minutes - first lesson free" or words to that effect. You could even use one of these brilliant giant aqua billboards: www.bbidisplays.com from the listing ahead on Page 191.

WEAKNESSES: Set-up costs with jet skis; insurance; maintenance; hungry sharks.

REAL WORLD BIZ: www.queenslandjetskihire.com; www.jerseyseasport.com; ww.goldcoastjetskihire.com.au; www.watersportshire.com

★ *(Meat) Pie Shop*

CONCEPT: For whatever reason, a good meat pie shop is actually one of the very best small businesses that any entrepreneur can start. Why? Repeat business is very strong; I have never seen queues stretching outside of *any* small businesses like pie shops and the formula for making a great pie is pretty straightforward. In a good location, a (meat) pie shop can make an exceptional living. Men especially love scoffing down a good meat pie.

STRENGTHS: See above

WEAKNESSES: Vegans won't be interested; you may develop an unhealthy addiction to your own pies but specialized counselling can overcome it; finding a good location and staffing.

REAL WORLD BIZ: www.upperkrustpieshop.com;

www.bigdadspies.com.au

★ *Buddhism Seminars*

CONCEPT: The Western interest in Buddhism has probably never been higher and individuals everywhere seem to be interested in learning more about this spirituality. Businesses that offer lectures, seminars and courses thus appear to be proving popular. A small business entrepreneur can also hire expert lecturers rather than necessarily being one themselves - though that should be a long term goal.

STRENGTHS: Buddhism is cool now; it's a really interesting philosophy; seminar/lecture/class venues can be hired on an *ad hoc* basis; spinoffs include selling books on Buddhism at your seminars.

WEAKNESSES: Not many; finding good lecturers until your own knowledge base has reached that level.

REAL WORLD BIZ: www.summerseminar.org; www.buddhism.hku.hk/WHATnews/Seminars/pastseminar.html

★ *Go-Kart Hire*

CONCEPT: This noisy but exhilarating small business actually encourages road rage, sort of, by hiring out motorised go-karts to driving lunatics to 'express themselves' on a track. Even corporations use these types of experiences for 'team bonding'.

STRENGTHS: Fun; 'adrenalinistic'; perfect for motorheads; novel experience.

WEAKNESSES: Cost of cars; cost of track; maintenance of both; licences; insurance; staffing; dead driver removals from the track can become tedious.

REAL WORLD BIZ: www.wannerookarthire.com.au; www.uk-go-karting.com/pages/fleet_hire.htm; www.cairnskarthire.com.au; http://ballarat.com/gokart.htm

★ *Mountain Bike Hire*

CONCEPT: Hire mountain bikes out to thrillseekers interested in tackling a nearby mountain run.

STRENGTHS: Outdoor work; fun; different kind of product/experience; opportunity to commercially monopolise a mountain.

WEAKNESSES: Seasonality; set-up with bikes; maintenance costs; any established competitors.

REAL WORLD BIZ: www.capitalbicyclehire.com.au; www.grizedalemountainbikes.co.uk/hire; www.afan-valley-bike-hire.com www.themountainbikehirecompany.co.uk;

★ *Mountain Climbing/Abseiling*

CONCEPT: With some outdoor background, a small business entrepreneur can offer classes and climbing and/or abseiling - possibly both on the one trip - in a spectacular local area.

STRENGTHS: Outdoors; exciting when you live - less so when death occurs; repeat business potential; the office views don't suck.

WEAKNESSES: Acrophobia; vertigo; possibility of gory, horrifying death; licences and permissions if needed; any established competitors.

REAL WORLD BIZ: www.rockfrog.co.uk; www.bcl.com.au/sydney/active/climbingabseiling.htm;

★ *Kayak Hire/Tours*

CONCEPT: At a local river/creek or waterside location, operate a kayak tour or kayak/canoe hire business.

STRENGTHS: Being outdoors; physical exercise; meeting new people on the tours; getting to know your local area more.

WEAKNESSES: Could be seasonal and restricted to warmer weather depending on your location; costs of kayaks; any established competitors; permissions and licences - if required.

REAL WORLD BIZ: www.seakayaking.com;
www.headwater.com/all/activities/canoeing.htm;
www.acadiafun.com

★ *Band Rehearsal Space Rentals*

CONCEPT: Every city has plenty of garage bands and
wannabe rockstars-in-training. However, a problem they
usually face is that their parents/neighbours will no
longer tolerate hearing *Smoke On The Water* at 200
decibels in their garage any more. The solution for them
is to rent out a space where they can rehearse - loudly.
Finding this kind of warehouse space isn't difficult and
free marketing via flyers in all of your city's music
instrument shops should ensure a steady flow of 'School
of Rock' graduates and drop-outs alike. Soundproofing is
a good, albeit costly, option too.

STRENGTHS: Apart from arranging the booking and
organizing the space, there is no actual labour involved;
cash-in-hand business.

WEAKNESSES: Finding a good warehouse/room space
to use that has reasonable transport access for starving
musicians; no other major drawbacks but make sure that
all bookings are paid for in cash - check for counterfeit
notes, you know what musos can be like.

REAL WORLD BIZ:
http://spotlightstudiosnw.com/rehearsals.aspx;
www.musicmakerstudios.com/practicerooms.shtml;
www.brockportstudios.com; www.bandname.com/
classifieds/

★ *Exotic Plant/Herb Dealer at Markets*

CONCEPT: Plant species like the Venus Flytrap, Cobra
Plant, Yellow Trumpet, Hooded Pitcher Plant and
Maroon Sundew Plant all like to eat. Meat. As such, they
are an intriguing novelty for children or childish adults

and can do very well at markets. Just keep your little children away from these carnivores.

STRENGTHS: Unique; novel; interesting; cheap to stock; impulse buying appeal to children - especially with live demonstrations where small animals are fed to them.

WEAKNESSES: Growing time; danger of attacking you.

REAL WORLD BIZ: www.petflytrap.com; www.buy-venus-flytrap-plants.com; www.urbanjungle.uk.com; www.davids-exoticplants.co.uk; www.theepicentre.com

★ *Vending Machines*

CONCEPT: One of the very best types of small business is one that requires the least amount of attention. Vending machines fit this model perfectly. Step 1: Purchase vending machine/s (or a vending franchise); Step 2: Negotiate with relevant businesses and organisations to use their space to place the machine (usually they will want a percentage); Step 3: Once/twice a week, you reload the stock and collect the profits.

STRENGTHS: Flexible hours; can be operated in parallel to a normal job while getting started; suits lazy entrepreneurs.

WEAKNESSES: Good locations are critical; purchase/franchise set-up costs.

REAL WORLD BIZ: www.vendingondemand.com; www.vendingmachinesunlimited.com; www.universalvending.com; www.generalvending.co.uk; www.ukvending.co.uk

★ *Skirmish/Paint-Ball Action Park*

CONCEPT: Indoor or outdoor, skirmish/paint-ball/laser-tag game centres have been around for a while and look like continuing to do so for a long time. That's why this type of small business is mentioned here. If there isn't one in your area and you feel the occasional need to release your inner Rambo in a non-violent way, sort of, then this option is worth considering.

STRENGTHS: Fun; repeat business probability; strong word-of-mouth potential; helps safely vent homicidal impulses in society.

WEAKNESSES: Set-up costs with indoor/outdoor venue - outdoor space would be cheaper (know any friendly farmers with a few acres to spare?); staffing; insurance.

REAL WORLD BIZ: www.skirmishsamford.com; www.skirmishuk.com; www.lasertag.com.au; www.darlingdownslaserskirmish.com.au

★ *Novelty/Fancy Dress Costumes for Kids (Online/Market Stall Sales)*

CONCEPT: As mentioned in several new small business entries here, those ventures that can appeal to impulse-buying spontaneity - especially with children - are usually on to a winning entrepreneurial formula. Look at coin-operated gumball machines, an ancient technology, but still profitable in 2008. Here, we are tapping into children's love of costumes and fancy dress, especially through a market stall where children can see, touch, and try on dazzling costumes.

STRENGTHS: Fun; spontaneous buying appeal; inventory not cripplingly expensive; use children you know for free market research; low cost of market stalls.

WEAKNESSES: It's a pretty childish small business for a grown-up, hang on, that could be a strength!

REAL WORLD BIZ: www.fancydress.com; www.allfancydress.com; www.joke.co.uk; www.pinkpineappleparty.co.uk

★ *Gourmet Ice Cream/Frozen Yoghurt Stand/Gelato Stall/Shop*

CONCEPT: Gourmet Ice Cream stores appeal to impulse-buying behaviour and thus can do very well in high traffic locations. They also offer novelty appeal compared to other fast-foods that consumers feel jaded with.

STRENGTHS: It's ice cream! Free samples; instant cashflow in right location; different; novel - especially with continual menu experimentation.

WEAKNESSES: Start-up costs; finding a great location; staffing; will it be a franchise or a 'copycat'?

REAL WORLD BIZ: www.valentinesicecream.com; www.honeysgourmet.com; ww.gourmeticecream.com.au; www.milwaukeejoes.com; www.chapsicecream.com

★ *$1/$2/$5/$10 Store*

CONCEPT: This small business revolves around a discount store where every single item inside is under $1 or $2 or $5 or $10. This can be operated as either a standalone venture, which is harder given the need to source all of the cheap inventory, *or* as a franchise where that side of the business has been sorted out. The websites below have more information on such franchises.

STRENGTHS: Virtually everyone wants a bargain - that's the principle that Wal-mart et al have built their entire empires on; cashflow from Day 1; dynamic business.

WEAKNESSES: Needs to be in a relatively high traffic area; high overheads including shop rental; staffing; low profit-high turnover business model.

REAL WORLD BIZ: www.poundland.co.uk; www.dollarstore.com; www.dollarstore.ca; www.dollaritem.com; www.dollardiscount.com

★ *Old-Fashioned Barber with Cheap Men's Haircuts*

CONCEPT: Men (especially older ones) want cheap, fast, no-frills haircuts. Even barber shops are franchised in today's franchise-mad small business world! Also consider variations where attractive women are the 'barbers', like the 'bikini car wash' business model as a point of difference.

STRENGTHS: Cash-in-hand business; social relationships with customers; repeat business potential – lifelong loyalty even - few businesses can offer that.

WEAKNESSES: Relies on high turnover and low cost rental in a high traffic area.

REAL WORLD BIZ: www.rudysbarbershop.com; www.vbarbershop.com; www.belmontbarbershop.com

★ *Gold/Gemstone Prospectors Store*

CONCEPT: A specialized store for amateur/semi-professional gold or gem prospectors. Many individuals enjoy this pastime as an outdoor hobby and are willing to spend considerable sums on getting the right equipment – dredges, metal detectors, sluices etc. One variation is to set up the business as an online store, possibly within eBay, even as a stepping stone to a 'real world' store.

STRENGTHS: Little or no competition if set up in the right area; lack of competition = greater profit margins; relationships with customers; word-of-mouth marketing potential; repeat business potential.

WEAKNESSES: Suits someone with interest in prospecting or knowledge of it; rental costs (unless operated online); inventory costs.

REAL WORLD BIZ: www.lifestylestore.com; www.armadillomining.com; www.abprospecting.com; www.modernprospector.com

★ *Private Tuition Centers*

CONCEPT: With the added academic pressure on children today, private teaching/tutoring on a one-on-one basis is booming. Centres where teachers and tutors can work privately with students with an emphasis on personal attention, flexibility to individual student needs (especially those with learning difficulties) are thus flourishing. Also check out the entry on private tutoring in the home on Page 220.

STRENGTHS: Good performance and word of mouth can allow premium pricing; teachers and tutors are employed on an hourly needs basis and are not a normal salary expense.

WEAKNESSES: Cost of renting a centre; possibility of centers existing in your area already; finding and keeping competent teaching staff – the same problem as many schools.

REAL WORLD BIZ: www.kumonedenprairie.com; www.aaatuition.com; www.firstclasslearning.co.uk; www.inspiretuition.org.uk; www.aim4a.com

★ *Car Valeting in Supermarket Car Parks*
CONCEPT: While shoppers shop at big, busy supermarkets, in the car park, their cars are being valeted or simply washed or cleaned at a certain agreed level of service. An agreement and fee will usually need to be paid to the supermarket in return for the 'use' of their customers.

STRENGTHS: Low start-up costs; outdoor work; no shortage of customers; repeat business.

WEAKNESSES: Negotiation necessary with the supermarket; business is weather-affected.

REAL WORLD BIZ: www.wavescarwash.co.uk

★ *Smoothie/Juice Bar Operator*
CONCEPT: In high traffic locations, fresh juice and Smoothie bars offer instant cashflow and plenty of retail action to a small business entrepreneur. According to Boost Juice, for example, their franchisees sell a collective total of 1 million juice drinks every month.

STRENGTHS: Dynamic; instant business when properly sited in high traffic area; small business 'footprint'; constant cashflow given its impulse-buying nature.

WEAKNESSES: Start-up costs; staffing; franchise costs if that option pursued (copying them and keeping all proceeds would be a better option).

REAL WORLD BIZ: www.boostjuicebars.com; www.vivajuice.com.au; www.originalsmoothie.com; www.juicejunction.com

★ *Personalized Mugs With Your Photo*

CONCEPT: From the UK, a company called Red Image have set up in high-traffic, shopping mall locations and offer mugs customized with images supplied by their customers - while they wait. They also offer wall sized canvas prints of images supplied in digital form by customers too.

STRENGTHS: Small business 'footprint'; impulse-buying appeal; great for gifts.

WEAKNESSES: The cost of setting up the business; staffing; getting a great location in a shopping mall that doesn't cost a ridiculous sum.

REAL WORLD BIZ: www.theredimage.com

★ *Umbrella Vending Machines*

CONCEPT: In rainy cities, vending machines selling cheap umbrellas are strategically placed to maximise the need for protection from the rain.

STRENGTHS: If located in busy subway stations, shopping or business areas, sales should be outstanding; owner does not need to be present to operate business; unique form of vending machine; no competition; more profit per unit sold than normal vending machine products.

WEAKNESSES: Dependent on rainy weather; the need to secure strategic locations for maximum sales; specialised nature of machines in terms of servicing.

REAL WORLD BIZ: www.umbrollys.com; www.umbrellabox.sg

~

~
14.
Home:
The Latest & Greatest
Small Business Ideas
That You Can Run
From Home.

~

★ *Experience Day Gifts*

CONCEPT: Like some others, the British company Prezzybox specialize in providing exhilarating or sensual one-day gift experiences. Apart from the novelty factor involved, overheads would actually be very low as venues and equipment would only need to be paid for on a per-job basis built into the charge to the client. Their brilliant gift experiences include: Hair & Makeover Experience; Paintball Experience; Introduction to Gliding; Health Spa Day for Two; Tank Paintball Battles; Dodgems Stockcar Racing; Ice Climbing; Mother and Baby Photoshoot; Wine Tasting at a Vineyard; Silverstone Ferrari 360 Experience; Interior Design Course; Powerboat Zapcat Blast; Ghost Hunting Experience; Indoor Bungee Jump; Double Decker Bus Driving; Feed the Big Cats Experience and many others. Such a business could be transplanted into almost any city in the world. Gold star for this small business!

STRENGTHS: Unique; fun; expandable; low overheads.

WEAKNESSES: Are there any?

REAL WORLD BIZ: www.prezzybox.com; www.intotheblue.co.uk (great range of experiences too!); www.incredible-adventures.com; www.giftybox.com; www.treatme.net; www.excitations.com; www.Opalroom.com

★ *Pick-up Artist & Mentor to Single Men/Women*

CONCEPT: Following on from the success of television shows like VH1's *The Pick-Up Artist*, books such as Neil Strauss' *The Game* and work in the field of dating by David DeAngelo, single men all over the world are rapidly discovering that being alone has nothing to do with looks, money or social status - in fact, it *all* hinges on social skills. While the aforementioned are doing well, the fact that over 50% of the population over 30 are now single and have been for some time indicates that a *lot* of lonely people are desperate to change their lives - just look at the phenomenal number of members on sites like Match.com. To this end, a small business entrepreneur could undertake an intense period of study - David DeAngelo (website below) is a fantastic starting point; David Shade is highly recommended too - and begin to personally mentor singles one-on-one in the local area on improving their social skills with women/men. 'Winging' with clients on nights out is also recommended. This is also an excellent business for women tutoring men in social attraction as proven by the success of www.thewinggirlmethod.com

STRENGTHS: Big potential client base in your area given the appalling rate of singlehood in our society and the fact that singles are now spending serious money on dating websites, and even cosmetic surgery to break out of their lonely lives; you can work from home so no office rental required.

WEAKNESSES: No income during research and skill development stage and expense of undertaking other singles social development programs and 'boot camps' of www.puatraining.com, http://realsocialdynamics.com.

REAL WORLD BIZ: See above websites plus http://doubleyourdating.com/0/Catalog/; www.davidshade.com

★ *Aqua Billboards*

CONCEPT: Billboards on buildings and beside busy roads are very old-hat now (hence rotating signs and trick special effects like those in London's Piccadilly Circus). Even billboard advertising on trucks - clever optical illusions mentioned on Page 97 notwithstanding - are also jaded. So how about big billboards in the water towed behind speedboats? See the pictures on the website below.

STRENGTHS: Novel; mobile; outdoor work; get a tan

while you work.

WEAKNESSES: Cost of boat; building up profile with advertising clients and outdoor media placement firms; sea-sickness?

REAL WORLD BIZ: www.bbidisplays.com

★ *Home Schooling Consultant*

CONCEPT: In the year 2005-2006, 1.9-2.4 million American children were home-schooled. However, parents considering this option for their children usually don't know how it all works - especially in relation to assessment and exams. As such, a local, knowledgeable Home Schooling Consultant can advise them. Home tutoring seems a natural spinoff business too - see the entries over on Pages 182 and 220 for more details.

STRENGTHS: Thriving market segment in education; possible long-term client relationships rather than one-off transaction; very low start-up costs; can work from home.

WEAKNESSES: If expanding the business, finding and keeping quality staff would be an issue - as it is for any business; constant research needed to keep up with examination requirements and ever-changing university admissions policies.

REAL WORLD BIZ: www.home-school.com; www.homeschoolcentral.com

★ *Cover Band Musician/Tribute Band*

CONCEPT: The Australian cover-band, Bjorn Again, an Abba tribute band, gross over 8 million dollars each year, mainly from touring. Other tribute bands, some of whom become fairly famous in their own right, do similarly well. Tim Owens, the singer in a well-known Judas Priest tribute band actually became the real band's lead singer in 1996. Other such tribute acts include Clouded House, the Pretend Pretenders, Pink Fraud and The Iron

Maidens. In short, a very good living can be made by a quality tribute band.

STRENGTHS: Great fun; still get the girls/boys like the real rock stars; musicianship does not necessarily need to be high as same repertoire is constantly performed; quick to establish if like-minded musician-entrepreneurs found.

WEAKNESSES: The musicians involved have to give up their desire to 'make it' as an original act; possibility of competing with other bands copying the same original outfit - though the world live band circuit is huge.

REAL WORLD BIZ: www.bjornagain.com; www.pinkfraud.co.uk

★ *'Green' Lawnmowing*

CONCEPT: Lawn care is big business. Countless franchises exist in the area and it is a tried-and-true small business. However, as our societal focus shifts to the environmental impact of our lifestyles, the demand for less ecologically-harmful products and services will continue. For example, Toyota sold over 180,000 Prisuses in 2006 globally and sales volumes continue to soar. Did you also know that 60% of water usage in the Western US states is expended on watering lawns? And that the EPA is planning harsh emission restrictions on conventional lawn mowers in the future? Therefore, a logical extension of this trend is the provision of 'green' lawn care services where non-polluting methods of lawn care are offered. One easy way to achieve this is through the latest versions of 'unmotorised' lawn cutting machines. Push/reel mowers are now relatively sophisticated and cheap compared to their counterparts of yesteryear and provide plenty of environmental 'feelgood factor' about the environment and even nostalgia for the past.

STRENGTHS: Outdoor lifestyle; exercise; suits

environmental focus of our times; low equipment and marketing cost to start; could be initiated as a part time business parallel to existing employment during start-up phase.

WEAKNESSES: Eventual proliferation of similar businesses.

REAL WORLD BIZ: www.planetnatural.com; www.peoplepoweredmachines.com; (these are sources of latest push mowers)

★ *'Green' Home Consultant*

CONCEPT: A knowledgeable consultant advises homeowners (renovating) or homebuilders on the latest and best environmentally friendly devices, materials and approaches to make their house 'greener' e.g. solar power, recycled/recyclable insulation materials. Homes actually emit more pollution over their lives than cars.

STRENGTHS: Few experts = high consultancy rates (supply/demand law).

WEAKNESSES: Advertising costs and time until critical mass established.

REAL WORLD BIZ: www.greenbuilding.com; www.sustainabledesignforum.com; www.buildinggreen.com; www.greenhomebuilding.com

★ *Grant Application Writer*

CONCEPT: Specialist writers of grant applications possess 'inside knowledge', research and copies of past winning applications (through Freedom of Information legislation) to assist new applicants, probably on a success fee basis. For example, in the UK, over £20 billion has been awarded to some 280,000 projects since 1994 (see www.lotterygoodcauses.org.uk). In short, writing grant application can be very lucrative.

STRENGTHS: A small percentage of a large grant can be a sizeable amount of money as remuneration; hardly any resources are needed apart from the ability to research and write in a professional manner; this is a vastly under-utilised field of writing and clients can use your services for life if your strike rate is sound (anything over 20% is fantastic); your fee could be a tax-deductible expense for your clients depending on local laws.

WEAKNESSES: Need solid writing skills; need to work on a success fee basis (no win, no pay) so have plenty of projects running at once; make *sure* that all arrangements are fully contracted and not simply verbal agreements.

USEFUL WEBSITES: www.grantsnet.org; www.lotterygoodcauses.org.uk; www.nsf.gov/funding/; www.srainternational.org/sra03/grantsweb/index.cfm; www.grantslink.gov.au

★ *Tender Writer*

CONCEPT: A tender writer is a specialist writer of tender/bid applications on behalf of small companies or businesses seeking to win contracts with government organisations or larger companies.

STRENGTHS: A small percentage of a large tender contract can be a substantial amount of money as remuneration; hardly any resources are needed apart from the ability to research and write in a professional manner; past winning and losing bids for government contracts can usually be viewed under Freedom of Information laws - this will be a guide on what makes a successful pitch and what fails; business can be operated from home.

WEAKNESSES: Like grant application writing above (why not do both and ghost writing from Page 198?), solid writing skills are essential; initially you will probably need to work on a success fee basis (no win, no pay) until you are established though this can be offset by a higher than usual fee if the tender wins; as above, make sure that such arrangements are fully contracted and not simply verbal agreements.

REAL WORLD BIZ: www.tenderwriting.com; www.writingbids.co.uk; http://tenderconsulting.com.au/index.htm; www.technicalwriter.com.au;

★ *Niche Caterer*

CONCEPT: Catering is a boom sector in small business. Find a form of catering that is not well...catered for and is interesting (e.g. Japanese, Vegan, Brazilian, Kosher) and establish a catering business *specialising* in that field.

STRENGTHS: Not easy for competitors to suddenly switch to another type of catering; raw materials can be purchased on a 'just-in-time' basis for specific jobs thus avoiding inventory expenses; good word-of-mouth builds fantastic catering business; can be run from home.

WEAKNESSES: Start-up period when clients are being acquired; building a reputation takes time - presence on CraigsList.org and in the Yellow Pages should help; vital to find and keep good staff through whom a reputation will grow or diminish.

REAL WORLD BIZ: www.sanilsell.co.uk; www.organikiss.biz; www.ramcaterers.com; www.easterncatering.co.uk

★ *Vineyard Tours*

CONCEPT: The hit independent film, *Sideways* illustrated the unique appeal of vineyards and the love of wine. If you live in or near an area populated by vineyards, consider offering tours of them including tastings.

STRENGTHS: Suits wine lovers; outdoor lifestyle; enjoyment of social interaction with clients; integrating with the wine-loving community; can pick up clients from central transit points and therefore may be able to run the business from home; senior-friendly small business.

WEAKNESSES: Requires living in or near a wine region; cost of vehicle/s; the need to establish relationships with existing vineyards; possibly competition from other vineyards already offering tours.
REAL WORLD BIZ: www.vineyardpartners.com; www.burdicktours.com; http://livineyardtours.com; www.sharpham.com/vineyard_tours.htm; www.corkd.com

★ *Gay Wedding Planner/Services*
CONCEPT: With laws across the Western world becoming more progressive in terms of same-sex legal unions, the demand for specialist gay wedding services grows. This small business type specializes in planning and staging weddings/civil services for gay couples.
STRENGTHS: Booming market as society becomes more tolerant; enjoyable social experiences sharing in couples' special day; good word-of-mouth and advance bookings can mean higher fees for services; can be run from home.
WEAKNESSES: Must suit owner's own moral views on same-sex marriage; excellent organisational and social skills needed.
REAL WORLD BIZ: www.pridebride.com; www.gayweddingsinscotland.co.uk; www.hudsonnuptials.com; www.alohamauigayweddings.com

★ *Online Background Checks*
CONCEPT: Companies are now emerging online that run various levels of background checks on individuals for different prices. In this way, companies can check on potential or existing employees, parents on their children's dates, landlords on potential tenants or anyone on anyone else. Given the increased desire for personal and commercial security, this is a booming field of

business.

STRENGTHS: Can be run from home; low set-up costs such as subscriptions to database services; doesn't require an extensive education/qualification process in a new area of knowledge (which many new small businesses do); senior-friendly small business.

WEAKNESSES: As the sector grows, more competitors will appear (though canvassing of local businesses should yield solid returns).

REAL WORLD BIZ: www.whoisshe.com; www.bestbackgroundchecks.com; www.backgroundchecks.com; www.quickbackgroundchecks.com

★ *Low-Cost Conveyancing/Property Title Transfer*

CONCEPT: Recognising that solicitors and attorneys had been charging excessive fees for decades for the legal transfer of property titles, savvy small business operators have set up their own (often online) one-price, low-cost alternative service. Depending on your territory's laws, law degrees may not be required and the business can be run online.

STRENGTHS: Online business should not require an office though canvassing of local real estate community will still be necessary; very low overheads.

WEAKNESSES: There may be competitors in your local area already which will lower profit margins; may require certain licenses and qualifications in your region; demands thorough knowledge and understanding of the property title transfer/conveyancing process; repeat business rare given the average purchase cycle of real estate buyers.

REAL WORLD BIZ: www.eliteconveyancing.co.uk; www.homelawdirect.ie; www.conveyancing-warehouse.com; www.cheapcheapconveyancing.co.uk

★ *Qualified Drug Tester*

CONCEPT: Increasingly, companies and organizations of all sizes are implementing random drug testing programs for their employees, especially as one means of avoiding litigation if an employee or worker harms a member of the public. To this end, small, highly-skilled drug testing businesses thus facilitate this growing trend.

STRENGTHS: Low overheads – the investment is in the qualifications and people; potentially very lucrative when ongoing relationships are established with large interstate/international businesses and organizations.

WEAKNESSES: Qualifications necessary; intense canvassing may be required at first.

REAL WORLD BIZ: www.drugstest.uk.com; www.avitarinc.com; www.employmentdrugtesting.com

★ *Personalized Printed Roses*

CONCEPT: PrintaPetal is a trademarked system for personalizing roses with specific, targeted messages printed on the flowers to add a special touch to celebrations. See the pictures on the website below.

STRENGTHS: Unique dealerships in each location; home-based; novelty for jaded consumers; senior-friendly small business.

WEAKNESSES: Check through contract with PrintaPetal thoroughly (like any business agreement); seasonal fluctuations like florists; repeat business cycle infrequent.

REAL WORLD BIZ: www.printapetal.com

★ *Green Courier – Toyota Prius Fleet*

CONCEPT: Green Express, a clever courier company from Atlanta, has implemented a Toyota Prius fleet whereby carbon emissions are greatly reduced and clients feel like they are making a small contribution to the green movement. While some pedants argue that diesel cars are more economical than the Toyota Prius, which they are overall, in congested, crawling, inner-city traffic, the Prius, and other new hybrids like it, use electric power almost *all* of the time and achieve around 40 mpg – something that no diesel can get near in those conditions in terms of emissions or economy.

STRENGTHS: Green power; positive free media attention; feelgood factor; point-of-difference from competitors; the vehicle can act as a moving billboard via magnetic signs.

WEAKNESSES: Eventually all courier companies will probably go hybrid or even lease fuel cell vehicles (a great option for a courier business too!); start-up costs of hybrid cars (leasing recommended for tax reasons).

REAL WORLD BIZ: www.greendelivers.com

★ *Self-Published Non-fiction Writer/Virtual Bookseller*
CONCEPT: Write and print – or use Lightning Source's excellent 'Print-On-Demand' (POD) Service at www.lightningsource.com - your own non-fiction books. Generally, the main inhibitor to publication and profits are large publishers, so cut out the publisher and retailers and go direct to the Internet – Amazon and Lightning Source (LSI) offers the greatest democratisation of book retailing ever. Must-read: *Aiming at Amazon: The NEW Business of Self Publishing* by Aaron Shepard. By scanning bestseller lists in your area/s of expertise, possible 'gaps' in the market should appear to you. Trivia: the book you are holding now and reading was created through Lightning Source's excellent 'Print-On-Demand' service.

STRENGTHS: No publisher to take majority of sales income; creative; satisfying; senior-friendly small business.

WEAKNESSES: Need for basic writing skills; you must edit and make sure your publication is as polished as possible; need to find a reliable printer – or use LSI's POD - for your books and ship books ASAP; you have to do most/all the things a publisher does - writing, editing, production, sales, marketing, distribution.

REAL WORLD BIZ: www.aaronshep.com (Self-Published Non-fiction/Fiction Writer); www.caiman.com (Virtual bookseller)

★ *Personal Counselling in Clients' Homes*
CONCEPT: After completing a necessary course for counselling accreditation, offer a counselling service in your area in clients' homes, where they feel more relaxed and talkative.

STRENGTHS: Offers major point-of-difference from all other types of office/clinic-based counselling; virtually no major start-up costs apart from study, targeted CraigsList.org, Gumtree.com classified advertising and Yellow Pages; satisfaction of helping your clients; intellectually interesting field of work; senior-friendly small business.

WEAKNESSES: Study and accreditation required; time needed to build business; may require some form of government licence in your area.

REAL WORLD BIZ: www.allpsychologyschools.com/faqs/become_counselor.php; www.instituteofcounselling.org.uk

★ *Provider of 'Butler/Maid-For-A-Day' Service*
CONCEPT: As a fun gift alternative, hiring a butler or maid for a day can be a thoughtful and surprising way to reward someone whose home duties are normally fairly demanding.

STRENGTHS: Very low overheads; mainly marketing and staffing; staff paid on a per-job basis; novel; fun.

WEAKNESSES: Making sure that staff perform to highest expectations; no other major concerns.

REAL WORLD BIZ: www.butlerforyou.com; www.personalbutlerservices.co.uk; www.amaidforaday.ca

★ *Last-Minute Child Care /Emergency Babysitting*
CONCEPT: Parents are occasionally or even *often* let down by babysitters who fail to turn up or call in sick. Rather than cancelling their plans, parents can instead turn to a small business that specializes in providing babysitting at the last minute – for a *higher* hourly fee.
STRENGTHS: Unique selling point; last minute = higher fees; huge client catchment; home-based means low overheads apart from marketing; staff paid on a per-job basis; senior-friendly small business.
WEAKNESSES: Making sure that your own sitters are reliable as it is your unique selling point; finding and keeping good reliable sitters.
REAL WORLD BIZ: http://lastminutebabysitting.com; www.news.com.au/dailytelegraph/story/0,22049,22988 430-5014717,00.html (don't you love how 'easy' some web archive addresses are?)

★ *Yoga/Salsa/Ceroc/Pilates/Ballroom/Tae-Bo Instructor or School Founder*
CONCEPT: Interest in dance-social-fitness activities like Salsa is presently huge across the world. In some areas, schools and classes have saturated an area whereas others don't seem to have many/any or good schools and classes.
STRENGTHS: Fun; social; friendships and relationships with clients; rent facilities on a per-class basis; great way to meet single women or men.
WEAKNESSES: Competitors in your area already established (though they may be complacent and poorly run); the need to become good enough to instruct or else hire instructors.
REAL WORLD BIZ: www.torontodancesalsa.ca;

http://salsadallas.com; www.salsaca.com

★ *Doula for Hire*
CONCEPT: According to the *American Heritage Dictionary*, a doula is "a woman who assists another woman during labor and provides support to her, the infant, and the family after childbirth." Approximately 4 million babies are born in the US every year so the need for maternal support is considerable.
STRENGTHS: Low overheads as marketing and study are the main expenses; relationships with mothers; word-of-mouth business among new mothers; emotionally rewarding; senior-friendly small business.
WEAKNESSES: Some study and qualifications such as Midwifery needed.
REAL WORLD BIZ: www.doula.com; www.doula.org.uk

★ *Specialist Classes for Disabled (e.g. Martial Arts, Archery, Pottery, Swimming)*
CONCEPT: Like the so-called 'able' population, the disabled love to participate in a broad range of sports, arts and recreational activities. With over *650 million* disabled individuals across the world, the market for such services is significant.
STRENGTHS: Fun; feelgood factor; positive local media attention; outdoors-based work; relationships with disabled and their carers.
WEAKNESSES: Not many – venues and equipment can be hired on an *ad hoc* basis.
REAL WORLD BIZ: www.disaboom.com/Living/; www.pyramid-of-arts.org.uk; http://news.medill.northwestern.edu/chicago/news.aspx?id=68923

★ *Storyteller for Hire for Kids' Parties/Events*

CONCEPT: The art of storytelling is captivating for children and even adults – as the success of audiobooks proves. Acting graduates/students from local drama college courses, for example, can be employed on a per-job basis to add live performance to children's birthday parties or even corporate events.

STRENGTHS: Low overheads; novelty; fun; good word-of-mouth marketing potential; senior-friendly small business.

WEAKNESSES: Business success depends on having several high-quality storytellers engaged by clients at once.

REAL WORLD BIZ: www.gigsalad.com/Actors-Actresses-Models/Storyteller; www.motell.org; www.storyteller.net/articles/81

★ *Mobile Car Repairs & Services*

CONCEPT: Like other new or newish small businesses mentioned in this book, bringing a service to customers at their home or work can create a winning business model. The concept of bringing automotive services to customers isn't new but it has proven to be a blue-chip, perennial small business type that can clearly be very lucrative if administered properly.

STRENGTHS: Various estimates suggest that there are up to 200 million cars in the US and over 32 million in the UK and they *all* need servicing.

WEAKNESSES: Mechanical expertise *or* the ability to manage and administer mechanics; considerable set-up costs.

REAL WORLD BIZ: www.mobileautoservice.ie; www.mobileproautorepair.com; www.mobile-auto-services.co.uk; www.emergencymobileautorepair.com

★ *Errand Service for Seniors*

CONCEPT: When the aging process inevitably sets in, running basic errands can become difficult for seniors. The small businesses below – see their websites – fulfil that basic function. Obviously our population is aging at a rapid rate so it is a growing market sector. The World Health Network estimates that by 2020, over 50 million Americans will be seniors over 65.

STRENGTHS: Low overheads apart from vehicle; home-based; relationships with seniors; potential for great word-of-mouth marketing; senior-friendly small business.

WEAKNESSES: Need to keep rates affordable - a flat fee is advisable; possibly the need to build business slowly, client by client and integrate these tasks into your efficiently organized daily routine.

REAL WORLD BIZ: http://errandsforseniors.com; www.errandservicebiz.com/seniors.html; www.errandsofthecarolinas.com/store.html

★ *Personal Trainer for Seniors (by them too) or Children*

CONCEPT: Seniors need to stay active in order to maintain their health and personal trainers specializing in this market sector can generate a successful business with word-of-mouth marketing among clients' friends. Even better, this is a great small business *for* an active senior who can train other seniors. Similarly, obese children often need the intervention of a personal trainer to overcome their unhealthy lifestyle. Consider personal training for the disabled too.

STRENGTHS: Active lifestyle; repeat business; relationships with clients; low overheads.

WEAKNESSES: Need for knowledge about health and fitness – knowledge that is constantly developing; need to stay in great shape as a role model for clients.

REAL WORLD BIZ: http://news14.com/content/ smart_woman/591733/personal-trainers-for-kids/Default.aspx; www.orlandopersonaltraining.com

★ *Mobile Beauty Treatment/Hairdressing*
CONCEPT: Bringing hair and beauty services to clients' homes rather than having them come to a salon or centralised location offers enhanced convenience and a significant point of difference. This is particularly beneficial for clients with mobility issues or overly busy lives and a higher fee can be charged given that they are being visited in the home.
STRENGTHS: Not many (any?) beauticians or hairdressers offer this service; very low start-up costs (no salon rental/staff hiring); word-of-mouth marketing can make business very lucrative; repeat business potential.
WEAKNESSES: Skill at hairdressing or beautician services needed but can be studied at local college; possible professional isolation; finding good staff when business expands.
REAL WORLD BIZ: www.hairathome.com.au; www.homehairdresser.co.uk; www.returntoglory.co.uk

★ *Prison Tours*
CONCEPT: In many countries, prisons are now privatised and run with a profit motive. In some of these prisons, tours are offered to those interested in a very *different* kind of sociological or cultural experience. Just as people are interested in watching a trial or parliament in action, curiosity does exist about prison life.
STRENGTHS: Unique; novel; unforgettable.
WEAKNESSES: Unique; novel; unforgettable; danger to tourists from inmates; keeping prison administration happy with the business; getting permission in the first place.
REAL WORLD BIZ: www.state.tn.us/correction/

institutions/tours/prisontours.html; www.dc.state.fl.us/oth/vtour/

★ *Haunted Tours*
CONCEPT: As tourists become increasingly jaded with run-of-the-mill tours, the demand for more visceral experiences grow. One way to harness that consumer desire for novelty is through staging tours of 'haunted' buildings in your area. Tours through Edinburgh's medieval underground vaults in Scotland, for example, are creepy – and popular (www.mercattours.com/haunted-underground-experience.asp).
STRENGTHS: Low overheads = high potential profits; word-of-mouth marketing potential; fun; scary; senior-friendly small business.
WEAKNESSES: Could be seasonal; negotiation with owners of 'haunted' sites for tour permission; competitors already established (research other atmospherically scary locations that they don't cover).
REAL WORLD BIZ: www.hauntedtours.com; www.hauntedvegastours.com; www.london-ghost-walk.co.uk; www.hauntedneworleanstours.com

★ *Home Handywoman*
CONCEPT: A great deal of market research clearly indicates that many women feel patronised by male 'technicians' and sales staff (especially in the automotive arena which is another small business opportunity). One powerful way to develop a business from this situation is to offer trade or general home repairs *by* women *for* women, 50% of the population.
STRENGTHS: More comfortable for women clients; novel; media attention; difference.
WEAKNESSES: Some trade skills required OR as the brilliant Brit Tina Huelin (www.handywoman.co.uk) proves below, the ability to *manage* such people –

recruiting from local trade colleges is one possibility.
REAL WORLD BIZ: www.handywomanri.com;
www.dorset-handywoman.co.uk;
www.handywoman.co.uk

★ *Fast, Affordable Home Inspections for Landlords/ Buyers/Sellers*
CONCEPT: Buyers/owners of properties need a fast, cheap, reliable inspection to ascertain the true physical condition of a house or apartment from an independent assessor, not someone with a potential conflict of interest. A flat-fee approach is recommended.
STRENGTHS: Can be operated from home; no provision of products therefore no inventory; sufficient expertise and experience should significantly speed up examination process; senior-friendly small business.
WEAKNESSES: Valuation knowledge needed and keen understanding of local market; low repeat business potential.
REAL WORLD BIZ: www.quadrantvaluations.com.au; www.distef.com

★ *Specialized Classic Car Restoration*
CONCEPT: As modern cars becoming increasing bland, many car buyers are chasing older classic cars in good condition. Demand for restored Nissan/Datsun 240Zs is very high (see www.geocities.com/~z-car/rebuild.html) but many other classics are also in very high demand when lovingly restored. Such in-demand cars include Jaguar E-Type (a recent UK *Daily Telegraph* poll winner of the Top 100 most beautiful cars of all time), older MGs, American classic 'muscle cars', Volkswagon Karmann Ghia Coupes and older Triumphs.
STRENGTHS: Potentially very good returns on each sale - the cars are limited in number so it's a seller's market (depending on the model); satisfaction of seeing

handiwork transform these cars; as the business and reputation grows, deposits can be taken on cars currently in progress.
WEAKNESSES: Cost of car purchase; cost and availability of parts; time needed to restore each car.
REAL WORLD BIZ: www.guildclassiccars.com; www.buyclassiccars.com; www.1inamillioncars.com; http://greatvehicles.chooseyouritem.com/classics/index.html; www.oldclassiccar.co.uk;

★ *Mobile Car Stone Chip Repair*
CONCEPT: ChipsAway, a British franchise, focuses on the mobile repair of stone chips on cars. Given the surging number of vehicles on our roads, there does not appear to be any shortage of customers.
STRENGTHS: Obvious demand for service; physical, outdoor work; expandability.
WEAKNESSES: Usual franchise issues especially the cost of holding the franchise; physical nature of the work (though this could be a plus for the right person).
REAL WORLD BIZ: www.chipsaway.co.uk

★ *Paparazzo*
CONCEPT: In certain locations, a good living can be earned by taking photos of celebrities. As such, this business type involves taking photographs of celebrities for newspapers and magazines.
STRENGTHS: High potential returns; exciting; enjoyment of star-spotting.
WEAKNESSES: Competition; ethically problematic; cost of specialized camera equipment.
REAL WORLD BIZ: www.spymedia.com; www.mrpaparazzi.com; www.thesnitcherdesk.com

★ *Weight Loss Buddy*
CONCEPT: TV shows like *The Biggest Loser* and

bestselling books like Dr Phil's *The Ultimate Weight Solution* illustrate how the chronically overweight struggle to overcome their destructive habits. A weight loss buddy – like a 'dive buddy' – mentors, guides, inspires and supports obese individuals one-on-one in their drive to reform their health.

STRENGTHS: Massive market sector given the Western world's obesity 'plague'; relationships with clients; low overheads; home-based; CraigsList.org and Gumtree.com are highly recommended advertising media; with a big number of clients mentored for 1-5 hours per week, this is a dynamite small business waiting to happen; senior-friendly small business.

WEAKNESSES: Nothing significant except for the 'buddy' to be fit themselves and have a good knowledge of health and diet.

REAL WORLD BIZ: http://burlington.craigslist.org/bts/546052289.html (illustrates need for Weight Loss Buddies); www.freedieting.com/weight_loss_buddy.htm; www.weightlossbuddy.com

★ *Small Business 'Renovator' or Makeover Mentor*
CONCEPT: As the business websites below indicate, there are two variations on this business. The first is as a small business consultant who assesses a small business's commercial 'health' – usually on a SWOT basis (Strengths, Weaknesses, Opportunities, Threats). This is partly what *E-Myth* guru, Michael E. Gerber, does and normally requires a good deal of small business experience. Another option is to look at poorly run businesses for sale in your area with a view, like a housing property developer, to buying, 'renovating' and re-selling that business. In fact, one of Michael E. Gerber's principles for small business success is to conceive your business as an entity being *prepared* for profitable sale within a specific time frame e.g. 3 years.

STRENGTHS: The small business earns revenue during the 'renovation', unlike a house redevelopment; exciting project-driven nature of the work – something that appeals to property developers; considerable profits if done properly; senior-friendly small business.

WEAKNESSES: High cost of small business purchase; intensive labour involved in 'renovating' that small business; reliance on favourable market conditions for sale.

REAL WORLD BIZ: www.businessweek.com/smallbiz/news/date/9906/f990625.htm; www.theapplegategroup.com/makeover.html; www.deluxe.com/small-business-makeover.jsp

★ *Rabbit 'Hotel' Owner*

CONCEPT: Jacky Hall, a British entrepreneur, recognized the need for the care of small pets, including rabbits, while their owners were away on holidays. To this end, she opened a very successful rabbit 'hotel' at her home. Her business is now being franchised nationally in the UK.

STRENGTHS: Dream job for pet lovers; great potential for word-of-mouth marketing; for someone with the land, the overheads are relatively low; senior-friendly small business.

WEAKNESSES: May only suit those with a large block of land; only suits pet lovers; pets will require constant supervision.

REAL WORLD BIZ: www.thebunnery.co.uk; www.smallanimalsboarding.co.uk

★ *Professional Mediators*

CONCEPT: Mediation is emerging as a constructive alternative to litigation and specialist mediators with a good reputation can earn a very good living. Study the websites below for examples of other practitioners in this field including how much they charge.

STRENGTHS: Training is not long compared to other fields and relies more on communication skills and empathy than endless degrees; can be home-based; very low overheads; easily expandable; a good relationship with one large multinational could provide years of work; no physical products required; senior-friendly small business.

WEAKNESSES: Strong communication skills are essential; study is required.

REAL WORLD BIZ: www.2mediate.org; www.mediate.com; www.arenamediation.co.uk

★ *Etiquette Training for Business*

CONCEPT: PR-conscious corporations are acutely aware today of the importance of interfacing with other businesses and the public in a professional and sophisticated manner. As such, they will often invest considerable sums in training their staff in forms of business etiquette. Some of the etiquette-based small businesses below also provide etiquette training for children and for international cross-cultural meetings.

STRENGTHS: No office required; like other specialized consultancies, one large corporation could provide many years of work; senior-friendly small business.

WEAKNESSES: High level communication and presentation skills essential; only suited to certain types of individuals; need for thorough, up-to-the-minute knowledge of etiquette.

REAL WORLD BIZ: www.etiquette-school.com; www.lettgroup.com; www.etiquetteexpert.com

★ *Online Tutor for 'E-Learning' in Remote Areas (Distance Education)*

CONCEPT: Distance education is big business and the Internet has, to a degree, reduced the isolation of those in remote areas wishing to learn. This is a business whereby a webcam and/or IM (Instant Messaging) is employed in order to facilitate one-one-one e-tuition/e-learning. Payment can be organized via PayPal. In short, it's tutoring, but online.

STRENGTHS: Very low overheads; flexible hours; CraigsList.org would be an excellent vehicle for advertising in targeted remote towns; senior-friendly small business.

WEAKNESSES: Requires experience in the relevant area of tutoring.

REAL WORLD BIZ: www.eden-online.org/eden.php; www.kwintessential.co.uk/online/language-tuition.html; www.acousticguitarworkshop.com; www.etutelage.com

★ *Birth Videography*

CONCEPT: Films like *My Life* with Michael Keaton in 1993 prefaced our desire to document every aspect of our lives in a way that Facebook and MySpace now reflect. One emerging area of 'self-life recording' is in the videography of a child's birth. HD camcorders and editing equipment, i.e. your PC, have never been cheaper, more professional looking or easier to use – Adobe Premiere, for example, is excellent and delivers very high quality results.

STRENGTHS: Being a part of an extraordinary experience; home-based; PCs are fantastic video editors now.

WEAKNESSES: Not for the squeamish; video equipment purchase cost; getting up to speed on using the equipment at a professional standard (there are no 'Take 2's' on this shoot!).

REAL WORLD BIZ: www.photo-talbot.com; www.davhouse.com/atr/about.htm

★ *Mobile Tanning Salon*

CONCEPT: UV-free tanning equipment is brought to the client's home for convenience and a clear point of difference from most other tanning salons is thus offered.

STRENGTHS: Cheap marketing e.g. CraigsList.org; repeat business; word-of-mouth marketing potential; machines do most of the work; it does not take many clients a day to have a thriving business; expandability.

WEAKNESSES: Initial equipment cost; training and qualification.

REAL WORLD BIZ: www.mobile-tan.com; www.athometanning.ie; www.technotan.com.au/international.php;

★ *Survival Training/Adventures*

CONCEPT: TV shows like *Man vs. Wild*, *Survivor* and the BBC's *Tribe* tap into an innate desire in some individuals to challenge themselves against nature. Interestingly, corporate 'team development' retreats – more like 'attacks' – also commonly focus on survival excursions. This small business lies in providing such experiences.

STRENGTHS: Outdoors lifestyle; relationships with clients; office can be based at home.

WEAKNESSES: Physically demanding; relevant background essential; competitors possibly already established in your area.

REAL WORLD BIZ: www.nwsos.com/wild.htm; www.bushcraftexpeditions.com; www.survival-school.org; www.boss-inc.com; www.buyagift.co.uk/Category/Id/1053/Name/Army_Skills

★ *Jobs Website For Ex-Military Personnel/Seniors*

CONCEPT: MilitaryExits.com specializes in jobs and employment listings for ex-military personnel. It is precisely this kind of targeted niche-industry building that a successful small business should seek to emulate. Consider a seniors/elderly-targeted jobs website too - hardly any competitors but worth the effort.

STRENGTHS: Home-based; word-of-mouth marketing potential; feelgood factor; positive media attention; senior-friendly small business.

WEAKNESSES: Smaller market sector but greater dominance of that sector.

REAL WORLD BIZ: www.militaryexits.com

★ *Doll Doctor/Doll Hospital*

CONCEPT: A doll doctor is someone who specializes in the repair and restoration of 'injured' dolls. This type of small business suits someone with a deep love of dolls and an aptitude for fine art.

STRENGTHS: Every area needs a doll hospital – does yours have one? Specialised craft = higher profits; suits doll lover perfectly; low overheads – home-based; this is one business that cannot be serviced very well online so local doll patients will need to visit their local doctor or doll hospital for emergency treatment; word-of-mouth marketing potential; senior-friendly small business.

WEAKNESSES: Not many but there may be competitors already established in your area.

REAL WORLD BIZ: www.dolldr.com; www.dolldoctorsassociation.com; www.dolldoctor.net; www.timelessdollhospital.com

★ *Driving Instructor for Disabled/Other Variations*

CONCEPT: Being a driving instructor is a pretty safe small business but what about narrowing that focus in order to dominate niche sub-segments. For example, why not, as illustrated on the websites below, target the disabled who are learning to drive. Other driving instruction variations could be woman-to-woman or migrant-to-migrant (same country of origin) driving instruction.

STRENGTHS: Blue-chip small business; word-of-mouth marketing potential; easy to finance given safety of this form of small business; senior-friendly small business.

WEAKNESSES: Cost of car; cost of car modifications for disabled; competition (hence the importance of niche variation); licensing requirements for instructor; thorough knowledge of road rules.

REAL WORLD BIZ: www.topclasstuition.com; www.americandrivingschool.com/disabled-drivers.html www.goldstardrivingschool.com.au/8.html; www.macquariedrivingschool.com.au/car-training/disabled.html

★ *Career-Change 'Test-Drives'*

CONCEPT: VocationVacations, an Oregon-based company, have innovated a new twist on career changing – they give their clients 'test drives' in' their dream jobs including mentoring, first-hand experience and contact-building in that profession. This market is wide open for similar businesses elsewhere. Given that most people change their careers three times during their lifetime now, a business like this can do very well. Brilliant.

STRENGTHS: Unique = higher profits; experiential; service-based so no products to bother with; senior-friendly small business.

WEAKNESSES: Unique = educating the market about this entirely new type of service; heavy reliance on word-of-mouth; demands excellent social and negotiating skills.

REAL WORLD BIZ: http://vocationvacations.com; www.figuringout.co.uk

★ *Gay & Lesbian Travel/Accommodation Review Website*

CONCEPT: *Pink Choice* is an American travel and accommodation review website that specializes in reviews *for* the gay and lesbian market and *by* them. In short, it's niche specialization. Possible variations on this small business are travel review websites for the disabled, adventure holiday lovers and women-oriented travel experiences (see entry way back on Page 165).

STRENGTHS: Potential dominance of a smaller, but still very lucrative, market sector; word-of-mouth marketing potential; income can be derived from booking fees and on-site advertising hence multiple revenue streams; enjoyment of working in a sector that the owner feels they belong to.

WEAKNESSES: As an online business, there are very few financial drawbacks; possibly only established competitors to challenge in target niche.

REAL WORLD BIZ: www.pinkchoice.com

★ *Performing Babysitters*

CONCEPT: Rather than providing conventional babysitters, Sitters Studio, a company based in New York and Chicago, provides trained entertainers to keep children, well, entertained. Parents can even choose the artistic discipline that they would like their sitter from e.g. painting, singing, dancing et al.

STRENGTHS: Unique; novel; fun; repeat business potential; fad/trend potential; word-of-mouth marketing potential; low-cost set-up.

WEAKNESSES: Need to educate the market; need to find babysitters who are both entertaining *and* good with children.

REAL WORLD BIZ: www.sittersstudio.com

★ *Shared Property Buying*

CONCEPT: Given the skyrocketing and often ridiculous prices of real estate in most major cities now (hello,

London!), one British company, Shared Spaces, has set up a facility for strangers to buy into property together, thus sharing the mortgage burden while allowing all parties to get on to the 'property ladder'.

STRENGTHS: Great idea; well suited to young urban buyers who could not otherwise buy property; everyone wants in on the property boom now; low cost to set-up as online venture in your area; can take small percentage of the sale price or flat fee to facilitate; senior-friendly small business - especially a senior with solid property buying experience.

WEAKNESSES: Inevitability of 'copycat' competitors – like all great ideas; need for every facet of the business to be contractually airtight; need to educate the market about this new type of service.

REAL WORLD BIZ: www.sharedspaces.co.uk

★ *Denim Doctor*

CONCEPT: For someone with sewing skills, offering 'denim therapy' to customers' tired old jeans could be a nice small business. As the company Denim Therapy below proves, people and their beloved jeans are not easily parted.

STRENGTHS: How many jeans are out there in the world today? Huge potential customer base.

WEAKNESSES: Need to educate the market about this type of service; requires relatively large number of customers for profitable business; low repeat business cycle likely.

REAL WORLD BIZ: www.denimtherapy.com

★ *Mattress Disposal & Recycling*

CONCEPT: Interestingly, one San Francisco company, BedBusters.com, specializes in just one aspect of rubbish removal: mattresses. As an added eco-twist, they take the unwanted mattresses to a recycling facility. Niche rubbish removal as a small business.

STRENGTHS: Mattresses are awkward and unwieldy beasts and clients will pay to be rid of these unwanted monsters; green angle; different; home-based so overheads low apart from suitable vehicle.

WEAKNESSES: Low repeat business cycle; cost of vehicle; getting and keeping strong, reliable mattress wranglers.

REAL WORLD BIZ: www.bedbusters.com

★ *Customised Storybooks Featuring…Your Child*
CONCEPT: Flattenme.com is an American company that specializes in offering a choice of 4 individual stories/storybooks that any child's picture can be integrated into, in order that she/he becomes the main character of that story. Digital printing technology obviously helps here in customising a beloved staple of childhood: the storybook.

STRENGTHS: Unique (so far); novel; fun – even suits as a humorous gift for adults; home-based for low overheads; senior-friendly small business.

WEAKNESSES: Need to educate the market – a market stall with numerous samples would help a lot.

REAL WORLD BIZ: www.flattenme.com

★ *Last Minute/Emergency Cleaning Services*
CONCEPT: Like the travel service LastMinute.com, a cleaning service that can be called upon in a crisis to take care of a cleaning job that simply has to get done offers a profitable small business model in its own right and a brilliant segue into lucrative long-term cleaning contracts.

STRENGTHS: Last minute emergency = higher charges; a professional one-off service for a client could lead to long-term cleaning work; cleaning small businesses have proven to be one of the most bullet-proof

and profitable of all the small businesses ever invented.
WEAKNESSES: Not many except the need for great staff to call on at the 'last minute'.
REAL WORLD BIZ: Several are listed on CraigsList.org (as you should if running this small business)

★ *eBay Consultant/Coach*
CONCEPT: With the surging interest among small business aspirants to get on to eBay - why not? - the parallel demand for coaching in eBay success has also grown. Such a business could easily be run online with webcams and IM (Instant Messaging) and very few practitioners exist in this niche one-on-one business coaching category so far – despite the relative abundance of books on the subject.
STRENGTHS: No products needed – service-based; global potential client base; still relatively untapped market = higher fees; eBay is hot now; senior-friendly small business.
WEAKNESSES: Requires an in-depth experience of eBay success and constant awareness of new developments in the way that eBay does business and any other relevant e-commerce developments.
REAL WORLD BIZ: http://zpg.ziply.com/zpg/us/ViewCA.php?idno=44700;
http://ebaysellingcoach.blogspot.com

★ *Amazon.com Consultant/Coach*
CONCEPT: As interest among aspiring writers and self-publishers grows in getting their products on to Amazon.com and its associated websites around the world, a clear need exists for one-on-one business coaching from someone who has been through the process successfully. For example, the must-have wisdom in the excellent book, *Aiming at Amazon: The NEW*

Business of Self Publishing by Aaron Shepard would translate brilliantly into personal Amazon success coaching – especially given that Amazon's businesses practices seem to be constantly changing.

STRENGTHS: Service-based hence low overheads; massive international potential client base; excellent potential returns from applying Amazon knowledge to a consultant's own books on Amazon; senior-friendly small business.

WEAKNESSES: Requires considerable first-hand experience of self-publishing success with Amazon and constant awareness of new developments.

REAL WORLD BIZ: Waiting for you!

★ *Christmas Tree Rental*

CONCEPT: While Christmas Tree rental has been common in the corporate sector for some time, it is now crossing over into residential homes where families are less comfortable with killing a tree each year. This type of business would work well in parallel with home Christmas decoration (especially the exterior decorating of family homes)

STRENGTHS: Eco-friendly; feelgood factor; should attract positive local media attention; could be run from a home with large area of land.

WEAKNESSES: Seasonal; space needed to grow and keep the trees.

REAL WORLD BIZ: www.livingchristmastrees.org; www.irishchristmastrees.com

★ *High School* Student Tutor in Students' Homes*
(*Tutoring for Entrance Exams into exclusive {private} high schools is also a booming sub-category).

CONCEPT: This small business involves academically competent tutors travelling to students' homes to coach them in high school subjects - depending on their individual strengths.

STRENGTHS: Home-based thus low overheads; virtually all income is in cash - taxation declaration is up to the individual entrepreneur; good hourly rates; working relationships with students can be very rewarding; word-of-mouth can build an excellent business - often with siblings in same house or nearby relatives/friends; good tutors can be booked ahead for years; senior-friendly small business for retired teachers.

WEAKNESSES: Some college qualification is obviously beneficial in convincing parents of suitability though even attendance at a teaching course may suffice; need for a reliable car; work is seasonal depending on school term dates; difficult to find other competent tutors to earn royalties from - the good ones have their own successful tuition businesses. See the center entry too on Page 182.

REAL WORLD BIZ: CraigsList.org (many examples there); for resource materials, try www.sparknotes.com; www.enotes.com

English High School Tuition
in your home!

EXPERIENCED TUTOR AVAILABLE
FOR AFTER SCHOOL/WEEKEND
ONE-ON-ONE ENGLISH & ESSAY
WRITING TUITION IN YOUR
HOME. REFERENCES AVAILABLE.
LIMITED PLACES.

$60 HOUR

PHONE **SUE SMITH** TODAY ON
XXXXXXXXXX FOR DETAILS.

★ *Custom/Artistic/Scented Candle-Making (for sales at markets/on eBay)*

CONCEPT: At markets, novelty items sell well and candles – which have a very strong appeal to women especially – can be easily customised to a variety of shapes and colours in a variety of substances – soy, for example. Such a business also translates well online as eBay's Hot Items Bestseller Lists at:
http://pages.eBay.com/sellercentral/hotitems.pdf
reveal the popularity of candles in that sales channel.

STRENGTHS: Impulse buy-oriented; cheap inventory; creative; women make up half the population; senior-friendly small business.

WEAKNESSES: Time needed to create candles, usually income only on market days, items are luxuries not necessities; skill-building required.

REAL WORLD BIZ: www.jaxcandles.com; www.caterpillarscandles.com; www.boysstuff.co.uk; www.kandlestixofoldtown.com; www.scentsationscandles.com (Check out their nifty "Heart-Shaped Chameleon Candles")

★ *Boarding/Rooming/Lodging House for Seniors*

CONCEPT: An unfortunate modern reality in our aging society is that many seniors do not have sufficient financial means to live comfortably in retirement. As such, many end up in rooming or boarding houses where they can only afford the rent on a small room in a large house with shared facilities. For the small business owner with a large house that can be converted into multiple rooms, this is a great cashflow business but is not suited to everyone's taste. Naturally, a boarding or rooming house open to all ages is also a viable small business.

STRENGTHS: Weekly/monthly cashflow; social relationships with tenants; feelgood factor from providing good standard of living and facilities for seniors; senior-friendly small business.

WEAKNESSES: Licensing requirements; adherence to all necessary safety and fire regulations – these are usually much more stringent than a normal suburban house; set-up costs could be considerable with house conversion.

REAL WORLD BIZ: Not really a web-friendly type of business but your local Yellow Pages or community newspaper should list some if you are curious about their charges and practices. This could be useful though: http://planmagic.com/business_plan/hotel/boarding_house_business_plan.html

★ *Business Computer Relocator*

CONCEPT: When businesses need to relocate, one specialized aspect of this move is the safe and orderly dismantling, transportation and re-installation of their computer systems. This is a very lucrative area of IT small business and for the tech-literate, an excellent potential small business.

STRENGTHS: Home-based; low overheads (apart from vehicles – which could be hired specifically for each job); networking opportunities with clients (no pun intended).

WEAKNESSES: Canvassing of businesses initially, Yellow Pages advertising essential including online + on Google; staffing; low repeat business cycle as businesses don't move that often.

REAL WORLD BIZ: www.pcdisconnect.com; www.sunspeed.co.uk; www.relocom.co.uk; www.chequerstransport.com/hardware_relocation/

★ *Tarot Card/Palm Reading*

CONCEPT: While clearly an 'old-school' type of small business, tarot card and palm reading is enjoying a resurgence of interest given the decline of Western institutional religion. If this type of small business interests you, a great deal of excellent reading material exists on the subject in addition to courses i.e. these are *skills* that can be learned and developed.

STRENGTHS: No product inventory; service-based; repeat business potential is strong; relationships with clients; senior-friendly small business.

WEAKNESSES: Competitors already established in your area (whom you should visit as a paying client to assess their services); need to spend time in study and skills acquisition.

REAL WORLD BIZ: www.thecrystaltarot.com; www.partypop.com/Vendors/4061648.htm; http://members.tripod.com/~atdaylong/

★ *Hot Air Balloon Rides*

CONCEPT: Not new (unless you also offer parachuting or bungee jumping from your balloon - some companies do!) but hot air balloon rides are still very successful if sited and marketed properly. Best of all, if heights don't terrify you, what a way to make a living?

STRENGTHS: The magnificent office views; sharing a great experience with your customers; great lifestyle.

WEAKNESSES: The terrifying office views; start-up costs; safety regulations, laws and licences; established competitors; possibly seasonal.

REAL WORLD BIZ: www.californiadreamin.com; www.adkballoonflights.com; www.canadahotairballoonrides.ca; www.balloonsoverbritain.co.uk

★ *Second-hand/Rare Vinyl/Rare DVD & CD Shop/Online at eBay & Amazon*

CONCEPT: Despite the iLife age we apparently live in now, there is still a niche demand for retro audio and video products. Such (Online?) shops offer interested buyers a different retail experience, especially when it comes to them discovering forgotten favourites and precious cultural 'artefacts' in these places.

STRENGTHS: Quirky; different; fun; suits retrophiles perfectly; repeat business potential; word-of-mouth potential.

WEAKNESSES: Inventory harder to acquire; normal retail presence issues e.g. location, staffing, overheads (could be avoided if operated online); may not necessarily be a massive money maker.

REAL WORLD BIZ: www.2ndhandtunes.com; www.moremusic.co.uk; www.beverlyrecords.com; www.audiophile-records.com

★ *Second-hand/Vintage/Specialist Car Hire Agency*
CONCEPT: Instead of competing head-on with big car rental firms offering bland, mass-market new cars, some small business operators offer vintage and classic cars for rent which offers a more romantic and unique driving experience, especially on a holiday or honeymoon. When you compare a Jaguar E-Type to, say a Hyundai Accent (sorry Korea), it's fairly obvious which one offers a more memorable experience.

STRENGTHS: Suits lovers of vintage and classic cars; different; fun; experience-based; senior-friendly small business.

WEAKNESSES: Older cars break down more and maintenance can be expensive; cost of inventory to hire out; insurance coverage; possible need for a site though could be done online with pickup at an agreed point e.g. hotel, airport or gas station.

REAL WORLD BIZ: www.classic-vintage-car-rental.com; www.motorclassic.co.za

★ *Unique Wedding Vehicle Hire*
CONCEPT: Like offering vintage, classic or exotic cars for rental (e.g. Pink Cadillacs, Horse & Carriage; White

1930s style cars like 'Great Gatsby'), renting out these types of cars for weddings or other special occasions is also a proven formula for small business success.

STRENGTHS: Families are willing to spend considerable sums on making a wedding day a unique experience - including the wedding fleet; being a part of special days.

WEAKNESSES: Established competitors; fleet cost; maintenance of older vehicles can be expensive; seasonal work; low repeat business cycle.

REAL WORLD BIZ: www.gatsbyscars.co.uk; www.classicelegancelimousine.com; www.classiclimos.com; www.american50s.co.uk

★ *Short Adult Course Provider (e.g. Cartography, Philately, Coins)*

CONCEPT: As the phenomenal success of self-help, DIY and non-fiction reference books proves (e.g. *Books for Dummies* and *Books for Idiots*), adults are now increasingly obsessed with expanding their skills and knowledge. Therefore, possession of a specialized skill or knowledge in a particular area can facilitate a small business based on running seminars in hired conference or college rooms. Advertising is through the usual channels recommended in this book on Page 83: CraigsList.org/Gumtree.com, local paper classifieds, A4 horizontal flyers placed in relevant sites, possibly DM letterbox drops (created on a PC of course), website keyword placement through Google e.g. "Denver lapidary classes", and relevant blogs or Yahoo community groups in that specific area.

STRENGTHS: Very low overheads; working with what you already have; social relationships with your students; senior-friendly small business.

WEAKNESSES: If you possess enough knowledge about an area or the passion to educate yourself, there are

very few downsides to this business except perhaps finding enough regular paying students from your catchment area to make this a lucrative venture - more expensive one-on-one tuition in your area is one obvious spinoff business.
REAL WORLD BIZ: www.cookitaly.com; www.nightcourses.com; www.schools.nt.edu.au/csc/NightClasses/courses.html; www.collageclass.com/college-night-classes.html

★ *Ghost Writer*
CONCEPT: Surprisingly, or unsurprisingly, many books are now not actually written by the person named on the cover. Why? Simply because that person might be an amazing snowboarder or footballer or pole-vaulter but can't tell a paragraph from a participle. To this end, the number of ghost writing 'gigs' available to those with some writing skill is quite big, especially in more mundane anonymous writing projects. Websites like Guru.com are one excellent way into this writing-related small business. A small business like this could be combined with technical writing from Page 232, tender writing from Page 194 and grant writing from Page 193.
STRENGTHS: Virtually no overheads; senior-friendly small business; repeat business potential when good name established.
WEAKNESSES: Writing skill required thus may suit retired/active teachers; hard to expand as a small business; social isolation hence the alcoholism of most great writers; constant deadlines.
REAL WORLD BIZ: www.guru.com; http://rentaghostwriter.com; www.gotdot.com/hire-a-ghost-writer.html; www.seo-writer.ca/freelance/ghost-writer.html

★ *Used Laptop/Notebook Dealer*

CONCEPT: Despite massive falls in the price of computer hardware in the last 10 years, students and those on very low incomes still struggle to afford computers, especially laptops/notebooks. Isn't a notebook made of paper? As a quick scan of eBay reveals, demand for cheaper laptops is strong. Second hand laptops can often be sourced from government/corporation auctions in job lots.

STRENGTHS: Good demand; big potential customer base with eBay; possibly a computer geek's dream small business.

WEAKNESSES: Unsold inventory; sourcing laptops cheaply enough to sustain profitability; unknown order of laptops bought in bulk from auctions; space needed for computer stuff - there *will* be complaints from the housemates; some technical knowledge of computers and their servicing is very useful; low repeat business cycle.

REAL WORLD BIZ: www.spintradeexchange.com/laptop-liquidation-liquidators.htm (for sourcing used laptops); www.usanotebook.com/news_page.php (again, for sourcing used laptops); try CraigsList.org for latest dealer ads.

★ *Local Fishing Tours*

CONCEPT: Using inside knowledge of fishing in the local area, fishing tours of secret 'hotspots' are offered to travellers - especially through flyers and a presence established with local tourism authorities.

STRENGTHS: Outdoor lifestyle; yummy fish for dinner; repeat business potential; what a way to make a living!

WEAKNESSES: If done with a boat (recommended), start-up costs are higher; working hours will include weekends and holidays; demands a deep knowledge of fishing idiosyncrasies in the local area and good social skills; fish sometimes bite back.

REAL WORLD BIZ: www.fishingthetropics.com.au; www.justfishing.co.za; www.randysfishingtrips.com; www.adamsfishingcharters.com

★ *Travelling Shows for Children/Elderly*

CONCEPT: Many small performance companies continuously tour with a group of niche-specific actors/musicians/dancers/performers. Actors or performers can be gained from placing notices up at local amateur theaters, music societies, conservatoriums and the like. Sample notice below.

STRENGTHS: Ideally, doing what the entrepreneur loves - performing, usually for a captive audience; low overheads apart from transport, great bonds develop between performers on the road; once a reputation is established, business blossoms.

WEAKNESSES: Initially, a great deal of correspondence and shoe leather to sell the show/s to organizations for children, the disabled (why not a show performed *by* the disabled *for* the disabled? That's real empowerment) and seniors.

REAL WORLD BIZ: www.bearspawgunslingers.com; www.aliveandkickingentertainments.co.uk/comedy/index.shtml; *For rates, actors union sites:* www.actorsequity.org (USA); www.caea.com (Canada); www.equity.org.uk (UK); www.irishactorsequity.ie (Ireland); www.alliance.org.au (Australia); www.nduunion.org.nz/actorsequity.htm (New Zealand)

See over for Sample Flyer:

Actors/Singers Needed!

TOURING COMPANY NEEDS
ACTORS AGED 21-35 FOR
COMMEDIA DELL'ARTE TOUR
OF STATE. <u>EQUITY RATES
PAID</u>. 6 MONTH CONTRACT.

PHONE **MIKE JONES** TODAY
ON XXXX XXXXX FOR
DETAILS.

★ *Premium Dog Walking Service*

CONCEPT: Like the Luxury Dog Washing business also featured on Page 243, walking the dogs of the rich can be an astonishingly lucrative racket, er, small business to get in on. Every day, the dogs of the rich need walking and often they do not have the time to do so. That's where a trusted, pet-loving dogwalker comes in. Positive word-of-mouth from one client can generate a full-time work load and many walkers take *several* dogs out together *at once*.

STRENGTHS: Suits an animal lover; high repeat business likelihood; strong word-of-mouth potential among affluent clients; senior-friendly small business.

WEAKNESSES: Finding and keeping other good dogwalkers who won't go and open their own dogwalking small business.

REAL WORLD BIZ: www.petaholics.com; www.angelasark.co.uk; www.doggywalker.com; www.alphadogwalkingservice.com

★ *Apartment/House Vacating Cleaning*

CONCEPT: Experienced landlords and property managers are increasingly building a contractually-binding, tenant-vacating clause into rental agreements whereby an agreed specialist cleaner performs a final cleaning service on a vacated apartment. The landlord/property manager is thus happy as the property is ready to be displayed at its best for the next tenant and the vacating tenant is happy as they will (probably) get back their full deposit/bond on the property given its good condition. By cold-calling every real estate agent and property manager in the local area, and nearby areas once the sales pitch is sufficiently 'tweaked', a solid cleaning small business can be built based on this subtle spinoff from the ubiquitous (and ubiquitously commercial) cleaning industry.

STRENGTHS: Low start-up costs; expandable; scalable from part-time to full-time (if you are renting, start with your own property manager/landlord with whom a relationship already exists); could be added to other cleaning small businesses like the one listed just back on Page 218.

WEAKNESSES: A fair number of real estate agents would be needed before business is viable; repeat business cycle around 6-12 months like rental lease agreements; quality staffing; cluttered market with cleaning businesses now; labor intensive.

REAL WORLD BIZ: See CraigsList.org for current ads in your area.

★ *Feng-Shui Consultant*

CONCEPT: If you have been living on another planet for the last 10 or so years, Feng Shui is the Chinese art of rearranging living spaces to maximize healthy 'energy flows' thus improving quality of life. Home remodelling enthusiasts use Feng Shui. So do massive corporations. If your preferred small business approach is to operate a consultancy, then Feng Shui is well worth a look.

STRENGTHS: Usual service-based small business benefits in terms of low overheads; hours; flexible; expandable; scalable from part-time to full-time; plenty of marketing options - think of property development media vehicles.

WEAKNESSES: You need a commercially acceptable knowledge of Feng-Shui principles, though this can be learnt through extensive reading and taking courses (practise on your relatives' homes!).

REAL WORLD BIZ: www.henryfong.com; www.fengshuili.com; www.fengshuiliving.com.au/ consultations.asp; www.sandiegofengshui.com

★ *House Staging/Dressing Business*
CONCEPT: House staging or dressing is the art of final preparation of a home for sale by meticulous maximization of its visual potential.

STRENGTHS: Rewarding; creative; artistic; project-by-project basis; word-of-mouth marketing potential; senior-friendly small business.

WEAKNESSES: Need for training; need for passion for house dressing; possibly established competitors.

REAL WORLD BIZ: www.stagedhomes.com; www.encorehome.com; www.stagingnewengland.com; www.home-staging-montreal.com

★ *Technical Writer*
CONCEPT: For those with developed writing skills and a logical, technically-literate mind, writing technical documentation is very much in demand. This type of business can work well in tandem with grant writing on Page 193, tender writing on Page 194 and ghost writing on Page 227.

STRENGTHS: Skill-based so no inventory required;

repeat business potential; experienced technical writers earn a very good living.

WEAKNESSES: Need for good writing and editing skills; technical documentation isn't the funkiest of topics to write about; nature of work isn't social; constant deadlines.

REAL WORLD BIZ: www.thewritersforhire.com/technical/; www.primewriter.com; www.idowriting.com; www.farbey.co.uk.

★ *Romance Novelist/Mills & Boon Writer*

CONCEPT: For those interested in making a living as a writer, writing short romance fiction novellas for Mills & Boon, Harlequin, Silhouette, MIRA and Steeple Hill books is very lucrative. To this end, extensive guidelines are available for new writers on the website below. Incidentally, romance fiction far outsells all other genres of books in the world.

STRENGTHS: Enjoyable for lovers of the romance genre; worldwide sales potential; home-based operation; part-time option at first.

WEAKNESSES: (Acquirable) fiction writing skill required; sporadic income; romance genre is not to everyone's taste.

REAL WORLD BIZ: www.millsandboon.co.uk (Site Map-Information for Aspiring Authors); www.lizfielding.com/tips.html

★ *Specialist Car Importer*

CONCEPT: A market has always existed for exotic and slightly unusual used cars for buyers with more individual taste in cars. Depreciation, the car importer's best friend, means that cars can be purchased in one territory, freighted to another and sold for a handsome profit. Depreciation, for example, in Britain is among the most severe in the world and cars imported from the UK to other right-hand-drive (RHD) markets can sell at a considerable profit. Possible car types: E-type Jaguar, XK Jaguar coupe (1997-2006), Nissan Skyline, Nissan 300ZX/350Z, Toyota Supra/Soarer, BMW M3/330 coupe/M5 sedan, Mercedes SL, older Porsche 911/928/ 944 Turbo/968, Ferraris. In short, a specialist car importer works out which territory across the whole world offers the most profitable importing opportunity and goes from there.

STRENGTHS: Great for car-lovers; unique cars = higher prices; can get big deposits or entire price for car before committing to importation; senior-friendly small business.

WEAKNESSES: Needs thorough understanding of importing process and legal car registration in target destination; sporadic earnings; time delays during import process - Buddhist patience recommended; yard or storage facility will probably be required.

REAL WORLD BIZ: www.japaneseusedcars.com; www.bestjapancar.com; www.1stcarimports.co.uk; www.euroimports.com

★ *Mobile Car CD Installation*

CONCEPT: Given the busy lives we all lead now, services that come to our car such as tune-ups, vehicle inspections and sound equipment/sat-nav installation are doing well.

STRENGTHS: Open-air profession (sort of); word-of-mouth marketing; relatively low cost set-up; relatively low number of installations required each week for healthy income; senior-friendly small business; the vehicle can act as a moving billboard via magnetic signs.

WEAKNESSES: Technical competency essential; ability to know or adapt to different car's idiosyncratic installation problems is important; business vehicle needed; relationships with product manufacturers will need to be established.

REAL WORLD BIZ: www.instaltech.bebo.com;
http://radio-waves.co.nz/

★ *Mobile Tire Fitting Service*

CONCEPT: Like other small businesses mentioned in this book, this service involves discounted tires brought to a customer's home and fitted there. Such a service adds considerable convenience and avoidance of boring time spent by customers waiting at a tire dealership.

STRENGTHS: Offers a clear point of differentiation from normal dealers; vehicle can act as moving billboard for the business; outdoor work.

WEAKNESSES: Tires are heavy and cumbersome to stock and carry around - best to buy inventory on-demand for specific jobs; specialized equipment needed; physically demanding job; competitive industry = lower profit margins.

REAL WORLD BIZ: www.etyres.co.uk;
www.thetirebrigade.com; www.roadrunnersonline.ca;
http://alltiresandrims2u.com/

★ *ESL Coach*

CONCEPT: We live in a globally dynamic world where tides of migration continue to flow towards the Western, 'First World'. In that world, English is obviously the dominant language and the more fluently a migrant of non-English speaking background can talk in English, the better their economic prospects are likely to be. As such, one-on-one ESL/EFL (teaching English as a Second Language/Foreign Language) tuition or in small groups can be a great way to make an independent living as a small business entrepreneur.

STRENGTHS: Relationships with clients, possibly lifelong as migrants do become attached to their 'link' between the two cultures; easy to find clients; senior-friendly small business; if teaching a small group, hire venues on an *ad hoc* basis rather than longer term arrangements; advertising on CraigsList.org and Gumtree.com highly recommended.

WEAKNESSES: Qualification beneficial and many accelerated TESOL/EFL/ESL options do exist.

REAL WORLD BIZ: www.englishtutorsydney.com; http://english-tutor-newton.bostoncatalog.com

★ *Letterbox Drop Supervision*

CONCEPT: DM, an acronym that stands for Direct Marketing and Direct Mail, is a very old form of business marketing. Think 'junk mail' through your letterbox. Any idea why companies still bother with this annoying 'mailbox spam'? Yep, it still works. And, DM companies need small business operators to supervise the thorough and reliable delivery of all that junk mail in *your* area. In this small business model, students, seniors and those 'between jobs' are usually employed on a per-thousand letterbox basis. So there aren't even weekly wages to pay. It may not be sexy. It may not be high-tech. It may not even be fun. But it is a proven, rock-solid small business.

STRENGTHS: Senior-friendly small business; not many big clients needed to generate serious income; expandable; strong repeat business potential - DM is delivered *every* day of the week.

WEAKNESSES: The need to monitor that your letterbox droppers are delivering the flyers and brochures as they are supposed to be (tell them that you have seven relatives on their route and will be checking that each of them received the materials); need for a big garage or workspace for all the advertising materials; finding and keeping reliable droppers.

REAL WORLD BIZ: Consult your local Yellow Pages for current advertising activity.

★ *Kite Building and Online Sales*

CONCEPT: Kites can be as distinctive as t-shirts and unique, visually striking kites can do very well via an eBay shop and/or beachside location in warm weather. Such positioning of kites is attempting to visually excite children into impulse-buying behaviour.

STRENGTHS: Fun; appeals to children; cheap to build; cheap to sell if working online; senior-friendly small business; easy to segue from part-time to full-time small business.

WEAKNESSES: Creative flair required; may be seasonal.

REAL WORLD BIZ: www.kite-sales.com; www.intothewind.com; http://yoyouniverse.com; www.lekite.com.au

★ *Newsletter Publishing*

CONCEPT: Niche newsletters can be very lucrative, particularly in fields related to wealth generation where the subscriber base has plenty of disposable income. Streetwise Publications in the UK (website below) is a perfect example of a very successful newsletter producer that targets, among other areas, British property speculators focused on Eastern Europe. Streetwise also advertises 'exclusive' reports that are widely advertised in Britain's newspapers. So what's your newsletter expertise in?

STRENGTHS: Information-based means no inventory or offices required (though Streetwise has offices as it has grown pretty big); senior-friendly small business.

WEAKNESSES: Building up your subscriber base will take marketing expenditure in relevant magazines, ezines and target-oriented sites; making sure that your research is up-to-date, thorough and valuable to your client base.

REAL WORLD BIZ: www.streetwisepublications.co.uk

★ Private Investigator

CONCEPT: Unlike Jim Rockford's beat-up trailer home in *The Rockford Files* would suggest, private investigation is a big, small business these days. With investigations ranging from possible insurance fraud to infidelity (50% divorce rates!), demand for private investigators is strong.

STRENGTHS: Service-based means no inventory; senior-friendly small business; expandable, especially with insurance companies as clients.

WEAKNESSES: Licence usually required along with some form of qualification; not suited to everyone's moral taste; no income during study and licensing phase; surveillance - unlike the movies - can be dreary even if you are being paid by the hour.

REAL WORLD BIZ: www.kaleinvestigation.com; www.interagencyla.com; www.investigators-private.com; www.demarr.com

★ Relocation Expert

CONCEPT: When executives move city, or country, many logistics need to be professionally organized and large companies are willing to pay handsome fees to make sure that the relocation needs of their management team are properly addressed. It's a fundamental part of keeping quality executives at a company.

STRENGTHS: Can all be arranged and organized from home; flexible hours; scalable and expandable business; small number of blue-chip multinational companies can provide an abundance of relocation business in our globalized world; senior-friendly small business.

WEAKNESSES: Established competitors - whom you can undercut or differentiate yourself from; demands highly organized and thorough individual with excellent social and negotiating skills.

REAL WORLD BIZ: www.simplysydney.com.au;

www.relocations-made-easy.com.au;
www.smoothmovessydney.com.au

★ *Prospecting Tours/Historical Tours*
CONCEPT: Organized tours of old historical and/or prospecting areas can be popular, if relevant to the local area. They do not require a retail office, just a great guide, coach (or offer walking tours) and permissions to conduct the tours. Such tours are of particular appeal to seniors.
STRENGTHS: Relatively inexpensive to set up; outdoor work; most areas have interesting histories if properly researched; hire of any vehicles or locations can be done on a per-job basis to keep overheads down; flyers, relationships with local tourism authorities and professional website should generate sufficient small business returns; senior-friendly small business.
WEAKNESSES: Possibly seasonal; repeat business unlikely given the range of travel options available in today's world.
REAL WORLD BIZ: www.miltours.com; www.goldrushtours.com.au

★ *Camp Variations for Children*
CONCEPT: Every year, literally millions of children go on different types of camps. That in itself is a cultural pattern that a terrific small business can be built on. But what about offering schools and parents in the local area different types of camp experiences e.g. environmental science camps, teenage entrepreneurs camp, drama camps, music camps, survival skill camps, camps for children with diabetes, weight loss camps for children and so on. All that is required is sound organizational skills and the confidence to market your camp concept.
STRENGTHS: Venues can be hired for camps as needed; staff - such as college teaching students - can be hired only as needed; memories of a great camp can stay

with a person for life; fun.

WEAKNESSES: Competitors - who are probably offering the same old type of children's camps; establishing your small business name for this type of camp in your local community; requires thorough logistic and planning capability.

REAL WORLD BIZ: www.adirondackcamp.com; www.wellspringcamps.com; www.manitoucamp.com ; www.childrenwithdiabetes.com/camps/

★ *Billboard On Your House/Property*

CONCEPT: For someone living on a busy road, it may be possible to get permission to erect a billboard on the property. Earnings then come from leasing the site to existing billboard operators or by managing it directly - starting with a sign reading "THIS SPACE FOR RENT PHONE 555-XXXX".

STRENGTHS: Business can be operated from home; very little effort required for the money earned after set-up; senior-friendly small business.

WEAKNESSES: Gaining permission to erect the signage is the biggest hurdle; it's a potentially ugly - but lucrative - addition to your property.

REAL WORLD BIZ: www.outdoorbillboard.com (to offer your space to)

★ *Ice Sculptor/Teacher*

CONCEPT: Who on earth would possibly want to learn how to make ice sculptures? Thousands of chefs and caterers, that's who. Providing someone has the skills and abilities to produce ice sculptures and can teach other people, then that individual has overcome the first hurdle in establishing a new business venture that teaches students how to make ice sculptures. Ice sculpture classes are best suited to being marketed directly to restaurant and catering company owners by arranging a presentation appointment to display and demonstrate the service. The business does not require an operating location, as the teacher can travel to clients' business locations and teach the ice sculpting classes on-site. This is an inexpensive business to establish and there should be no problems charging high hourly rates for these 'cool' specialized services. In fact, this small business has two revenue streams: the making of ice sculptures for clients e.g. weddings, Christmas parties; and the aforementioned teaching of ice sculpting.

STRENGTHS: Visually striking end results; teaching provides steady cashflow while sculptures for parties and restaurants can add revenue/profit spikes; inventory cost is low as it's...ice?; good word-of-mouth potential.

WEAKNESSES: Requires tactile artistic ability; time needed to establish critical commercial mass and profile.

REAL WORLD BIZ: www.ice-impressions.com; http://jrsice.com; www.icesculpture.co.uk; www.icecreations.co.uk

★ *Personalised License Plate Speculator/Dealer*
CONCEPT: In an age where more and more people seek to individualise their identity via tattoos and body piercings, custom licence plates are increasingly desirable. In 2005 in Hong Kong, one license plate sold for US$900,000. The main costs of the business are plate purchasing and advertising. You could also form business relationships with prestige car dealers in your area and notify them of plates that you have featuring their brands – they receive a small commission for connecting you with their new Porsche/Audi/BMW/Mercedes/Lexus/Ferrari buyer especially by keeping the 'finger on the pulse' of new premium models in the pipeline e.g. Audi Q5, Q3 and TTS, Porsche Panamera, Aston Martin Rapide and the BMW X6.

STRENGTHS: No office premises required; some plates

command small fortunes (why not advertise in magazines that the rich/aspiring frequently read?).

WEAKNESSES: Initial phase of self-education necessary; some plate configurations might be a riskier buy than others; may be other competitors already established in your area.

REAL WORLD BIZ: www.greatplateexchange.com; www.autoplates.com; www.no1showplates.co.uk

★ *Freelance Fundraising Consultant*

CONCEPT: Skilled fundraisers are in high demand so if you have excellent networking and social skills, this could be a very lucrative small business. Watch out that satisfied clients don't try to take you on full-time as this might limit your earning potential.

STRENGTHS: Potentially high returns; home-based business; endless repeat business for a talented fundraiser.

WEAKNESSES: Early clients are harder to get than later ones; ability to network essential - local community associations are an indispensable starting point; every aspect of the business must be scrupulously legal and transparent.

REAL WORLD BIZ: www.pfconsultancy.co.uk; www.lmarshallfconsultancy.co.uk; www.tlfc.org; www.dmi.co.za

★ *Debt/Credit Counsellor*

CONCEPT: The simple fact is that most people are drowning in pointless consumer debt these days - much of it on 'junk' credit card expenditure. Debt counselling is thus emerging as one spinoff small business industry that helps guide the debt-addicted into financial health.

STRENGTHS: No shortage of potential clients; low-overheads; satisfying helping clients get control of their lives back; senior-friendly small business.

WEAKNESSES: Heavily indebted clients may not make the most reliable payers for your service; convincing people overwhelmed by debt to spend money on *another* service; need for some form of counselling qualification (even if the exact solutions can be found at www.moneysavingexpert.com and in books like those of Dave Ramsey in *The Total Money Makeover: A Proven Plan for Financial Fitness* and Martin Lewis in *The Money Diet*)

REAL WORLD BIZ: www.cambridge-credit.org; www.incharge.org; www.credit-counseling-solutions.com; www.moneymanagement.org

★ *Medium/Psychic for Hire*

CONCEPT: A significant niche audience exists that is intrigued by the paranormal, fortune telling, numerology and other associated realms of knowledge. If you are intuitive, interested in human psychology and comfortable with this form of small business, word-of-mouth can make this a very successful operation.

STRENGTHS: No inventory; reasonable repeat business expectation; relationships with clients; meet clients at a local coffee shop or at home; one chatty satisfied client can generate plenty of business; highly profitable.

WEAKNESSES: Is it real?; not suited to the sceptical; could be a crowded market where you live.

REAL WORLD BIZ: www.psychicsforhire.com; www.dragonflypsychic.com/hireme.html; www.gigmasters.com/Psychic/Psychic.asp

★ *Mobile Luxury Dog Washing*

CONCEPT: This small business involves washing the dogs of rich or rich-ish people. Also check out the new dog washing vending machine on Page 141 and dog walking on Page 230.

STRENGTHS: Repeat business potential; relationships with clients; relationships with dogs; low set-up costs; expandable; vehicle acts as a giant billboard for the business - a 'dog van' like the one in *Dumb & Dumber* perhaps?

WEAKNESSES: Main one would be established competitors but there are a *lot* of dogs to go around. Woof.

REAL WORLD BIZ: www.cleandognow.com; www.heidismobilepetgrooming.com

★ *Domain Name Trading/Cybersquatter*

CONCEPT: Yep-still! Depending on the cyberlaws of the territory where you live, there is still a potentially good living to be made from acquiring web domain names that have not yet been registered. This is best done either by registering domain names - a small financial gamble in itself - when named new products are in the 'pipeline' e.g. PS4.com or PS5.com, MacbookAir.co.uk - *or* by registering names in non .com territories e.g. ipod.ch, blu-ray.com.au *or* by tieing up blue-chip brand names on newly released web suffixes - .biz and .info are recent additions to the web lexicon. With these names, examine up-and-coming/forthcoming: band names, car models, technological products, fashion labels, TV shows, movies et al.

STRENGTHS: Virtually no actual labor involved; each domain name is cheap to tie up if not owned by someone else; potentially very lucrative.

WEAKNESSES: Every name bought is a gamble on future demand; in the US, knowledge of the Anti-cybersquatting Consumer Protection Act (ACPA) and the Uniform Dispute Resolution Policy (UDRP) is essential but many companies can't be bothered with the delay of court action and will simply buy the cybersquatter off; competitors after relatively small number of domains.

REAL WORLD BIZ: www.ozdomainer.com; www.ricksblog.com

★ *Home Renovation Planner/Project Manager*
CONCEPT: Home property development or remodelling is actually considerably more complex than many amateurs realize until it is too late and many expensive, avoidable mistakes that *could* have been avoided were not *avoided*. A growing band of experienced remodelling/property project managers are thus emerging who take care of the owner's complete development – for a considerable fee. Oh and by the way, home renovation is a $350 billion+ a year industry in North America.
STRENGTHS: May be possible to manage several projects at once using same trustworthy tradespeople; expandable business; can get management fee in advance.
WEAKNESSES: Detailed understanding of logistics of property development and remodelling are essential; strong interpersonal skills and management essential; some clients can be indecisive, change their minds constantly mid-project or just be generally difficult.
REAL WORLD BIZ: www.renplan.com

★ *Cold-Call Training Service*
CONCEPT: Given how many businesses rely on the seemingly ancient art of 'cold calling' – unsolicited attempts to sell products and services – coaching individuals within those companies in the necessary skills and tactics to cold call effectively seems one corporate coaching small business that will probably never go out of style.
STRENGTHS: Virtually no start-up costs; repeat business potential – one big corporate client would be enough to sustain a very lucrative business; expandable; portable; mobile.

WEAKNESSES: Demands sales background and knowledge of the cold calling-sales process; best suits an assertive, confident individual with high-level communication skills who is also comfortable in a crowd.
REAL WORLD BIZ: www.accelerated-sales-results.com

★ *Loft Converter*
CONCEPT: One aspect of modern property development that maximizes a property's room and value, especially in places where space is at a premium (Good morning London and New York!), is to convert a loft into a proper living space in the form of an extra bedroom. Some canny homeowners even do a loft conversion, add an external staircase and rent their converted loft out as a separate flat – thus adding hundreds of dollars to the household monthly income.
STRENGTHS: With a solid reputation, good loft converters are booked out years ahead; word-of-mouth potential; renovations can be paid for up front by the client thus easing cashflow concerns; expandable small business.
WEAKNESSES: Suits someone with a building background or in managing tradespeople; cost over-runs if misquoted; demands strong project management skills and client negotiation abilities.
REAL WORLD BIZ: www.loft-conversions.com; www.econoloft.co.uk; www.uk-loft-conversion.com; www.loftconversionwarehouse.com

★ *Skip Hire*
CONCEPT: With the tremendous amount of small-scale property development and home DIY going on now, one need that certain small businesses cater to is the need for leftover rubbish to be stored and dumped via 'skips' a.k.a. 'dumpsters'. Clients pay for the 'skip' hire, permit for its

temporary placement on their street and removal. Apart from the delivery, pickup and dumping (days/weeks/months later), there isn't much labor involved – just the right equipment. This small business may sound complicated but it isn't and a small business that specializes in skip hire can do very well.

STRENGTHS: Huge demand for this type of service – is there anyone *not* developing their property now? Basically, this is a truck driving small business with plenty of time spent out of the truck while clients fill the skips; through cheap magnetic signs, the truck is a giant billboard for the small business.

WEAKNESSES: Specialized truck lease/purchase; skips; knowledge about street permits; arrangements for legal, safe emptying of skips afterwards.

REAL WORLD BIZ: www.topskips.com; www.skip-tip.co.uk; http://zbestrubbishremoval.com; http://trashbegone.com

★ *Infant/Toddler Equipment Rental*

CONCEPT: Given the rate that young children outgrow equipment that is necessary to their safe transportation and general comfort – high chairs, strollers, cribs and so forth – it makes more sense to rent out this equipment as needed rather than buying. That is precisely how the businesses below operate. One variation on this small business is to offer rental of this equipment to families vacationing in your area.

STRENGTHS: Considerable pool of potential customers; good repeat business potential; word-of-mouth marketing; cheap to market well (see relevant chapter in this book, *25 Great Places To Freely/Cheaply Advertise Your Small Business* on Page 83); senior-friendly small business; possibility of partnerships with family-oriented hotels.

WEAKNESSES: The need to educate the market about

this type of service; inventory costs; inventory maintenance; damage to inventory.

REAL WORLD BIZ: www.weetravel.ca; www.thetravelingbabyco.com; www.babyequipmenthire.com.au.

★ *Mobile Alloy Wheel Repair/Detailing*

CONCEPT: Car-based small businesses are usually winners. Here, it's a mobile alloy wheel repair service. As most modern cars have aesthetically pleasing alloy wheels, kind of, the potential customer base is pretty large. Can be operated as a franchise or standalone/copycat.

STRENGTHS: Multiple businesses based on alloy wheels: repair, polishing, straightening, remanufacturing, sale of new wheels; word-of-mouth potential; working outdoors; satisfaction of seeing positive results of work.

WEAKNESSES: Demands comfort working with cars or managing those who do; skill and knowledge is needed for alloy wheel repair; low repeat business cycle; set-up costs e.g. vehicles, tools.

REAL WORLD BIZ: www.mobilewheelrepair.biz; *Car Detailing:* www.mobileworks.com; www.superiorshine.com; www.detailking.com; www.nationaldetail.com

★ *Junk Removal*

CONCEPT: *1-800-Got-Junk* has over 300 franchisees and has apparently enjoyed 500% growth over the past 3 years. *College Hunks Hauling Junk* is another similar business that's pure junk. Copycat business anyone?

STRENGTHS: There's a hell of a lot of junk out there - too much, in fact; plenty of potential clients in our consumption-driven society; expandable.

WEAKNESSES: Franchise cost and/or vehicle; staff - college 'hunks' perhaps?; competitors.

REAL WORLD BIZ: www.1800gotjunk.com; http://1800junkusa.com

★ *Mobile Retro Experience Pizza*

CONCEPT: Another interesting pizza variation out there is a hire-able, fully restored 1946 truck, a 'Big Green Truck' (see pictures on website below) which adds a nice sense of nostalgia to any outdoor event where pizza-lovers congregate.

STRENGTHS: Unique; novel; fun; impulse-buy oriented; repeat business potential; word of mouth potential.

WEAKNESSES: Start-up cost of modified van; normal staffing issues.

REAL WORLD BIZ: www.biggreentruckpizza.com

★ *Used Musical Instrument Dealer*

CONCEPT: eBay's Hot Items list (bestsellers) at http://pages.eBay.com/sellercentral/hotitems.pdf proves that there is a pretty significant market for used musical instruments. If music is one of your passions, being a dealer in such instruments could be a lucrative side or even primary business. If you are wondering where to source such items, ask eBay's established sellers by posing as an interested buyer who is concerned about where the item came from and its history. By revealing this information to you, you too can source instruments there. This could also be a healthy spinoff from a music tuition small business, like the 'School of Rock' small business on Page 169 or the band rehearsal room small business on Page 178.

STRENGTHS: Relates to music - it beats selling life insurance!; very low overheads if conducted online and/or from home; fun.

WEAKNESSES: Slow selling inventory - that's why keeping a close eye on eBay's hottest sellers at the above web address is essential; established competitors in your area.

REAL WORLD BIZ: www.elderly.com; www.palmguitars.nl; www.daddys.com; www.usedmusicalinstrument.com; http://pages.eBay.com/sellercentral/hotitems.pdf

★ *Human Billboards*

CONCEPT: 'Human billboards' are individuals employed to wear 'mini-billboards' or placards while walking around in people-intensive areas e.g. office areas during lunch and train stations in peak hour. They are a quick, cost-effective way for a company to get a message in front of their target market. Students, homemakers or seniors looking for a little extra cash can be easily recruited - CraigsList.org or Gumtree.com is a great place to start recruiting. Staff should be trained and ideally interact with the public in a friendly, possibly humorous way. In terms of attracting paying advertisers, this can be done through cold calling, local paper advertising, a letterbox DM campaign to local businesses and by joining your local business group e.g. Chamber of Commerce or other body that attracts business owners.

STRENGTHS: Very low start-up costs; staff paid on a per-job basis or as percentage of the advertising contract; repeat business potential; high profitability potential.

WEAKNESSES: Need to aggressively market the service to local businesses; time to build up critical mass; suits a confident, assertive type of personality.

REAL WORLD BIZ: www.displays2go.com/product.wide.asp?ID=9142

★ *Mobile Car Upholstery Repair*

CONCEPT: As stated in other small business entries in this book, any entrepreneur targeting cars can often do very well given that there are so many of them out there and they all need maintenance of some sort. This particular small business type focuses on repairing worn and torn car upholstery and could suit a senior particularly well.

STRENGTHS: Millions of cars = millions of potential customers; mainly service-based and home-based so overheads are pretty low; profitable; enjoyable seeing results of labour; relatively quick to acquire skills.

WEAKNESSES: Requires skill in the process of car upholstery restoration - but this is a very learnable skill; normal need to educate the local market about your presence through local paper, DM letterbox campaign and Yellow Pages (especially the online version); low repeat business cycle; appropriate vehicle required that can act as a mobile billboard for the business (a clean, used van in good condition would be perfectly adequate).

REAL WORLD BIZ: www.playerautointerior.com; www.autoleatherrepair.com; www.trim-tech.co.uk

★ *Chuck Wagon/Mobile Food Concessions*
CONCEPT: A 'Chuck Wagon' or mobile food concession is a mobile provider of fast foods that can be temporarily set up near a major sporting event, concert, worker-heavy industrial area, public gathering or busy roadside. One parallel small business could be the portable toilet hire business on Page 140.

STRENGTHS: Great cashflow business; can make a lot of money very quickly at the right venue; chuck wagon can be parked at home to reduce overheads; different; mobile; able to maximize opportunities quickly e.g. near a political rally that has just been relocated to a different park.

WEAKNESSES: Start-up costs; maintenance of the chuck wagon; staffing; permission/permits.

REAL WORLD BIZ: www.californiacartbuilder.com; www.lisasconcessions.com; www.tandcconcessions.com;

www.mobilecateringbusiness.com

★ *Double-Decker Bus Tours*

CONCEPT: Tourism is an industry that continues to grow every year as the world becomes increasingly affluent and more of the world opens up to tourists - even trips to Antarctica are now 'normal'. One proven winner to tourists visiting a new city is the English-style, open double-decker bus. Being open allows for brilliant visibility and the driver also serves as a tour guide during the trip. Anyone who has been to Manhattan knows how popular these services are. A spinoff business could be making the bus/es available for charter by companies or other organizations. Is there one in your area?

STRENGTHS: Expandable; different; fun; good cashflow business during the busy season; possibly bus can be kept at home to lower overheads.

WEAKNESSES: Seasonal business; start-up cost of bus; maintenance costs; getting permission; staffing.

REAL WORLD BIZ: www.inetours.com/New_York/Tours/DD_Bus_Tour.html; www.theoriginaltour.com; www.bigbus.ca; www.city-sightseeing.com

★ *Military Memorabilia/Medal Dealer*

CONCEPT: There exists a considerable demand for military memorabilia and this is illustrated by its inclusion on eBay's Hottest Selling Items list at http://pages.eBay.com/sellercentral/hotitems.pdf If this area of collecting and selling strikes a chord with you, this is a strong niche small business to consider. Obviously other collector's items like coins, foreign currency notes and stamps also do very well and should be considered.

STRENGTHS: Appeals to a certain kind of collector/entrepreneur; historical interest; can be run online as an eBay shop so overheads are very low; repeat business

potential; senior-friendly small business.
WEAKNESSES: Sourcing profitable memorabilia; building up knowledge base about area of memorabilia (niche-specific books obviously help).
REAL WORLD BIZ: www.wwmeinc.com/store/; www.arbeia.demon.co.uk/srs/collect/milsig.htm

★ *Anger Management Counsellor*
CONCEPT: The world today makes many people pretty angry and even court judgements can now *insist* that people get anger management therapy. Therefore, those interested in counselling-style small businesses should consider specializing in this area of counselling. With the right qualifications, classes can also be organized for adult groups which should prove a profitable spinoff.
STRENGTHS: Service-based; no inventory; potentially long client therapy cycles (years?); relationships with clients.
WEAKNESSES: Need for qualifications; time taken to build up clientele; dealing with angry people.
REAL WORLD BIZ: www.angeronline.com; www.phoenix-counselling.co.uk; www.conflictcenter.org/classes/index.htm; www.andersonservices.com

★ *Novelty T-Shirt Maker*
CONCEPT: Threadless.com, a Chicago-based t-shirt maker specializes in making off-the-wall t-shirts for a young clientele. In so doing, they appeal to a young, impulse-buying oriented market where t-shirt use is very high. Such a business can be replicated elsewhere.
STRENGTHS: Cool; fun; offers individuality to business and consumer; imaginative; repeat business potential; word-of-mouth potential; could work well for a market stall; potentially very profitable.
WEAKNESSES: Inventory needed - though online business would only require one actual t-shirt in each size

to be made; requires creativity; possibility of being stuck with inventory that doesn't sell but low per-unit cost should make this bearable.

REAL WORLD BIZ: www.threadless.com

★ *Chef-For-A-Day*

CONCEPT: Like a *Maid-For-A-Day* service, the provision of a qualified chef to cook for a special meal at home with a partner or a corporate event is a fun novelty. Best of all, a service-based business like this can be run from home.

STRENGTHS: No inventory required as it is service based; employed chefs can be paid on a per-job basis; novel; fun; nice gift idea; word-of-mouth potential.

WEAKNESSES: Need to educate the market about this new type of service; need to find several quality chefs to build business (local hospitality college graduates, for example); business build-up may take time.

REAL WORLD BIZ: www.privatechefsinc.com/ day.htm; www.findgift.com/gift-ideas/pid-63888/; www.iglou.com/restaurants/chefforaday.shtml

★ *(Mobile) Foot Masseuse/Masseuse*

CONCEPT: According to APMA, the American Podiatric Medical Association, up to 75% of Americans will experience a foot problem during their lifetime. For such individuals, an expert foot massage in their own home is extremely appealing.

STRENGTHS: Ultra-low start-up costs; service-based; word-of-mouth marketing potential; relationships with clients; repeat business; well suited to advertising on CraigsList.org.

WEAKNESSES: Training required for qualification; feet can smell - ewwww!; only suits those comfortable working with the human body.

REAL WORLD BIZ: www.footnurse.com

★ *Aztec/Incan Jewellery Store (Online)*

CONCEPT: Niche jewellery always performs well as a small business. To this end, beautiful, affordable Incan and Aztec jewellery is sourced and sold either through a market stall or online (an eBay shop, for example, would be very straightforward).

STRENGTHS: Niche; visually different; beautiful; cheap inventory; senior-friendly small business.

WEAKNESSES: Low repeat business cycle; high turnover needed with lower price items; inconsistent income if operated as a market stall - unless it is in a 7-day-a-week market.

REAL WORLD BIZ: www.aztecjewellery.co.uk; www.incazone.com

★ *'Scooterman' Drunk Driver Service*

CONCEPT: From Britain comes a new franchise operation whereby clients make a booking for a 'Scooterman', a rider on a small folding scooter, to meet them at a pub or party, put the folded scooter in the boot of the client's car and drive the (slightly drunk) client home in her or his car.

STRENGTHS: Plenty of drinkers around; overcomes the need for a 'designated driver', franchise offers a set territory.

WEAKNESSES: Eventual copycat competitors; scooters are not very masculine to be seen on; normal franchise issues.

REAL WORLD BIZ: www.scooterman.co.uk

* * * * *

Phew! If you've made it this far and *still* haven't found a great small business to actively pursue, or had a spinoff idea from one of these, then perhaps the 2009 edition of this book will help! As I said at the beginning of this book, all of the most brilliant ideas, knowledge, secrets and approaches in the world are worth absolutely nothing without one thing:

the will to *Act*.

Happy trails!
Terry Kyle
Editor

~

~
15.
50+ Brilliant
Web Resources
for
Small Businesses.

~

Small Business E-Zines

www.entrepeneur.com

www.inc.com

www.businessownersideacafe.com

http://smallbusinessreview.com

www.3gsem.com
(Search Engine Marketing news)

www.springwise.com

www.fool.com
(Investment news & advice)

New Product & Small Business Ideas Sites

www.stupid.com

www.findgift.com

www.boysstuff.co.uk

www.firebox.com

http://dvice.com

www.coolhunting.com

www.coolest-gadgets.com

~

New Product & Small Business Ideas Sites

www.popsci.com

http://gizmodo.com

www.kilian-nakamura.com/catalog/index.php
(Japan Trend Shop)

www.ubergizmo.com

www.thinkgeek.com

www.grand-illusions.com

www.21stcentury.co.uk/gadgets/

www.trendhunter.com

www.trendwatching.com

http://vat19.com

www.lighterside.com

http://getsilly.com

www.boysstuff.co.uk

www.iwantoneofthose.com

www.discoverthis.com

www.spilsbury.com

~

New Product & Small Business Ideas Sites

http://inventorspot.com

www.perpetualkid.com

http://charlesandmarie.com

www.uncommongoods.com

www.newlaunches.com

Small Business Support Resources

www.entrepreneur.com/ebay/index.html

www.entrepreneur.com/franchiseopportunities/
index.html

www.irs.gov/businesses/small/index.html
www.business.gov

www.nfib.com

www.allbusiness.com

www.entrepreneur.com/ebay/index.html

www.allbusiness.com

www.score.org

www.vfinance.com

~

Small Business Support Resources

www.garage.com

www.businessfinance.com

www.freelawyer.co.uk
(Free UK legal advice)

www.zoho.com
(Free business software)

www.nolo.com

www.smallbusiness.com
http://sbdcnet.org

www.business.com

http://smallbusiness.aol.com

www.businessfinance.com
(Small Business Loan Search Tool)

www.startups.co.uk

Franchise Information

www.franchisedirect.com

www.thefranchisemagazine.net

www.thefranchisemall.com

~

Franchise Information

www.franchisegator.com

www.franchisedirect.co.uk

Advanced Search Tools

www.clusty.com
(better than Google?)

www.mamma.com/psearch.html
(Searches all major engines at once)

www.keyworddiscovery.com/search.html
(Keyword popularity tool)

www.salesrankexpress.com
(Amazon.com sales ranks)

www.metacrawler.com
(Searches major engines simultaneously)

Miscellaneous

www.videojug.com
www.wonderhowto.com
(Great range of free instructional videos
including aspects of small business)

www.infectedornot.com
(Free virus checker for your computers)

~

Miscellaneous

www.moneysavingexpert.com
(UK-focused but principles are universal)

http://babelfish.altavista.com
(Language translation online in real time)

www.xe.com/ucc/
(International Currency Exchange Calculator)

www.wikipedia.org
(Add an entry on your small business
that search engines will pick up and show)

www.hypertemplates.com
www.templatemonster.com
(Excellent range of web page templates to buy or copy)

www.zoopla.co.uk
(Free online UK property valuations for specific
addresses)

www.carbonneutral.com
(Free carbon footprint calculator)

~

~

16.
Small Business 'Micro-Mastery':
100+ Winning Tactics That Could Save
You From Small Business Bankruptcy.

~

Without wishing to overindulge in hyperbole, these simple *un*common-sense 'micro-mastery' small business tactics constitute some of the best wisdom about small business ever devised. In fact, following these principles in your next small business could be *the* difference between success and failure, high-fives or suicide hotline calls, lemonade or lemons. Need I go on?

* * * * *

A fact that that many companies and especially governments stupidly neglect is that any institution is only as good as the people actually running it. The best equipped, highest-tech, shiniest, swankiest office complex in the world isn't worth a damn if it's occupied by talentless hacks. That's why investment in the salary of a terrific staff member is far wiser than expenditure on 'bricks and mortar' - just look at the hordes of talented teachers streaming out of education every day because of the miserable salaries and absurdly unrealistic workloads. Can government leaders get any more short sighted on this issue? Don't let the same distorted priorities affect your business.

* * * * *

In your business, try to create 'disciples' rather than 'terrorists'. 'Disciples' are people who are very happy with your service and tell their friends. 'Terrorists' tell their friends that doing business with you was terrible. In time, this word-of-mouth can either expand or destroy a business.

* * * * *

When hiring, look for talented human beings more than those with extensive experience in a particular area. Quality people can learn to do almost any job quickly. Such people will enrich your business with who they are *as human beings* more than as experienced employees.

If you employ several people in your small business venture, always be willing to pitch in on the most menial, dirtiest job without complaint. Totally avoid the 'I'm above that kind of work' mentality which can alienate employees and create a management/worker divide. True leadership is about leading in *any* situation - without being obsessively controlling!

* * * * *

Try to develop multi-skilled employees. This gives you greater flexibility in a crisis when people are ill, on leave or otherwise unavailable. It also makes work less monotonous for employees if their skills are developed beyond one function.

* * * * *

Avoid borrowing money to set up a new small business - a true value small business should be possible in financial terms organically rather than with a giant expenditure initially. Negotiate on everything and don't ever let vanity dictate *any* expenditure!

* * * * *

If a small business is built on impulse-buying, e.g. a gelato stand in the town square, that customer impulse *must* be satisfied quickly. The 'buying temperature' of impulse purchases cools *very* rapidly and if not quickly fulfilled, potential customers will soon move on.

* * * * *

When running an online business, always communicate with your clients. People need to trust those with whom they deal with. The internet takes away reassuring 'face-to-face' contact, so you must make up for this with quick, direct lines of communication. Fast e-mail replies to customer correspondence should thus be an unbreakable commandment.

* * * * *

Like diet and exercise for human bodies, think of the necessary elements of a healthy business 'body'. Such ingredients include objective audits and reviews, materials and equipment used, physical business layout (if relevant), staffing levels, staff morale, staff relationships, ongoing innovation and analysis of costs.

* * * * *

Always consider the worst case scenario of your business decisions before committing to them. If that worst case scenario is bearable, then proceed. If not, then more fallback options need to be devised as safeguards e.g. building a small business up while still keeping the 'day job'.

* * * * *

Ensure that all of your business materials have a consistent, professional appearance. Every letterhead, business card, web page (within your whole site), fax cover sheet, envelope and bag must reinforce the professionalism of your operation. Far too many businesses have solid paper materials but an appalling website or the reverse (or neither!). It isn't good enough and it's amazing how poor and amateurish the business materials of many large multinational corporations are. Don't make the same mistake.

* * * * *

Try to subtly encourage your customers to see you as a partner in their business (or life too) - not just someone they occasionally buy a product or service from. With sincerity and a genuine interest in their goals, they could potentially be a lifelong customer delivering continual repeat business.

Don't treat your small business as a hobby. Treat it as a *way of life* or part of a way of life - your *chosen* way of life. Something that is only a hobby will always remain small. But something that is part of your way of life will probably last and develop.

* * * * *

Different prospects react to different tactics. Don't be too pushy with those who don't like it and press with those who need it. This should become intuitive after dealing with enough prospects.

* * * * *

If you address normal sales inquiries fast, try to answer complaints much faster. The single most common grievance that consumers have about businesses when a complaint arises is how slow the firm was in responding. Consumers take it personally when there are long delays in correspondence.

* * * * *

Always know exactly what price, product and service your competitors are offering. Ignorance of this 'business intelligence' can quickly cost sales and prospects. Always try to add more *perceived* value to your service or product than your competitors.

* * * * *

Always try to keep your price points below certain psychological thresholds. Retail stores have always done this and probably always will because it works. $99.95 sounds and feels lower than $100. It's 'counter-intuitive' and shouldn't make any difference but it does.

* * * * *

Rather than presenting fiddly, itemised accounts that are generally irritating to buyers, try to create 'all-inclusive' deals where 'one price fits all' - if possible. For some clients, this may involve more time than others but no buyer likes unexpected surprises in their bills. For example, many attorneys will charge $500 an hour and then add $1.50 for photocopying on top of it in itemised bills. Such an approach alienates buyers/clients and damages good will. Try to conceive your business as a kind of game - within which there are many secondary 'games' - wherein both winning and losing take place. This approach can help keep the inevitable lows in perspective and keep your desire to 'play' strong.

* * * * *

E-mail is a terrific, cost-minimal mechanism for communicating with clients and prospects - provided that someone in your operation has the time and social skills to answer messages promptly (under 24 hours is good, under an hour during business hours is better). E-mail costs nothing and shows your clients how 'on the ball' you are and responsive to their needs. I have lost count of the number of times I have made an e-mail sales enquiry to an established business only to receive no reply and shop elsewhere. Like katas in karate, a great small business performs certain repeated commercial sequences with absolute precision.

* * * * *

Always carry business cards (with your up-to-date details of course). You never know when someone will ask for one and it could lead to much more business. Writing your number on the back of a beer coaster - even really artistically - doesn't have quite the same professionalism.

* * * * *

Learn about your clients. A friendly chat isn't just a pleasantry, it is also on-the-spot market research. You can quickly learn their likes and dislikes, whilst also gathering information. This way you can alter your sales pitch for more effective results in the future.

* * * * *

Always maintain eye contact with people. It shows that you are not only attentive, but implies an honest temperament, strength of character and reliability.

* * * * *

In Microsoft Word, create a one-sided or two-sided A4 'mini-catalogue' of your products or services which can be inserted into bags or other materials that clients or customers receive. By doing it in Word and printing on a quality, textured paper, you are saving a fortune on graphics and printing and 'road testing' different campaigns for next to nothing and with instant flexibility. Your mini-catalogue could even feature one 'doorbuster' special product on one side and a bigger range on the flipside.

* * * * *

Try to remove as many obstacles - perceived and real - between your prospects' interest in your product/service and crossing the line to buy. Asking prospects and customers can help as does the input of staff. For example, sweet financing deals are one way that car dealers use this principle every day.

Build a profile as an expert in your small business area and enhance that profile through local media. Community papers (e.g. an expert 'Q & A' column), radio and possibly TV are good places to start and your small business will be associated with your expertise and thus be trusted more by prospects.

* * * * *

If there is ever a dispute with a customer over a purchase, offer an immediate, unconditional and totally courteous refund. It is *never* worth the ill-will or time to not offer this to a customer and the number of buyers in this category is always very, very low. A genuine and immediate offer of refund is professional; bickering and arguing is not.

* * * * *

One truism in small business is that the longer an account is unpaid, the more likely it is that it *won't* be paid. Be proactive and follow up *all* overdue accounts with friendly, courteous reminders.

* * * * *

Bill or invoice *immediately* upon delivery. It's staggering to find that many small businesses - especially busy ones - are lazy and slow in their invoicing! That's money that should be in their bank account within the agreed number of days. Even worse, such sloppiness runs the risk of losing track of money owed altogether. Furthermore, clients will have moved out of the phase where they remember how much they needed that product or service and are now *much* less motivated to pay promptly. 'Striking while the iron is hot is not only a cliché' but should be a *strict* commandment for all small businesses.

* * * * *

Aim to be methodical and consistent in your work habits. Even though there is now no boss looking over your shoulder and checking when you punched in, disciplined work habits and boundaries are still essential. In Richard Templar's thought-provoking, *The Rules of Wealth*, his Rule #5 is that those who do succeed constantly work their socks off and are thus more likely to be rewarded by their various initiatives. Simple and obvious but how much time in our lives is wasted, for example, watching lousy TV?

Work from a 'To Do' List each day that was compiled at the *end* of the previous work day. There is no point trying to construct one on the morning of that day - too many things are likely to be forgotten. In this way, each day feels solidly productive and gives a sense of real momentum.

* * * * *

Spell things out. Both staff and prospects/customers who don't have your expertise in your chosen area won't 'join the dots' as quickly as you. Be patient and always use concrete examples not abstract statements e.g. X brand modem allows you to send an average photo or home video over the net in about 30 seconds as opposed to X brand modem has a baud speed of 950 'jagigawatts' per teraflop.

* * * * *

Sell your belief. When you are in business, the art to converting a customer is to sell to them *your* belief in your product or service. It's contagious. The best salespeople can do this without even believing in their product or services, though of course authenticity helps.

* * * * *

Despite the boom in women-centered consumer products, many stores and products still fail to be female friendly. That's around 50% of the population ignored. Preposterous! Always remember to cater to *both* sexes, if relevant for your small business.

* * * * *

Always be friendly. It may be obvious, but how many times have you been to a store and have met abrupt, rude staff. Chat with your customers, treat them as people not targets. They'll notice the difference.

Never lose your cool. No matter how incompetent or negligent a person is, do *not* get angry. What does anger ever achieve? How does it rectify the process? How does it appear to others? Will it be beneficial for your health? It's just plain professional to treat *everyone* with dignity, no matter how big a mess they might make.

* * * * *

Don't make a big business decision without sleeping on it. It's surprising how a good night's sleep helps objectivity and clarity and may help to avoid a decision that is regretted later.

* * * * *

Proper preparation is *the* key to later success. Any small business venture should begin with several months of documented, detailed planning and research. Research and commercial intelligence gathering - most of which is free - can make all the difference in the world.

* * * * *

View every day in your business as a new opportunity to fine tune, tweak, develop, or experiment with some minor enhancements. Many businesses have suddenly made a vital change one day to suddenly discover the missing 'X Factor' in their operation. At the worst, it will add drive, energy and freshness to the 'vibe' your business puts out.

* * * * *

If relevant for your type of operation, send all your clients hand-written Christmas cards thanking them for their business.

* * * * *

When purchasing a small business, consider that the notion of 'Goodwill' is rarely that and is often the opposite.

* * * * *

Rather than always trying to reach single buyers, try working with another business to reach a larger group. For example, instead of a cleaning company trying to attract individual homes or businesses, it could try to build a relationship with a property management firm responsible for the care of hundreds of properties.

* * * * *

Set deadlines. Without them, most human beings won't work towards anything concrete. At times they may need to be flexible but at other times, not so. Like a daily 'To Do' list, it keeps momentum going forward for you *and* your business. Similarly, never let staff loaf around feeling bored. It's a terrible energy that 'pollutes' the atmosphere of a work environment. Workers should be constantly active; otherwise the need for them seems questionable.

P in a meaningful quote to your computer or office door. Such inspirations have a way of being absorbed into our ethical life. A good list for inspiring business axioms can be found right here in this book in *The Best Quotes of All Time About Business* back on Page 63.

* * * * *

M ake sure that your family and/or partner are *fully* informed about your small business aspirations and the impact that it will have on your lifestyle. If they are fully informed, they are more likely to support you in the changes - few people like change - and in the inevitable 'bad times'. When a business venture isn't performing, it can be far more stressful when those around us appear unsupportive.

I f you will spend long hours in an office in your small business venture, then make sure that you put *your* stamp on that space. It should be a place that you feel physically and emotionally happy in for long stretches. If that means that Hendrix is playing loud and the walls are bright pink, so be it. After all, being in a position to make these choices was part of why you started your own business in the first place, wasn't it?

* * * * *

O wn up to your own mistakes. Always. It's a tremendously liberating character trait to develop and frankly the only way to live. One of the sad indictments on our times is the lack of accountability or ownership that individuals are willing to take for their actions. Rather than perpetuating this childish culture of blame, admit your mistakes, apologize and move on. If you act out of a genuine, sincere motivation, your reputation will be greatly enhanced.

* * * * *

While being cautious and thorough is prudent, too many of us are timid in pursuing things that we really desire. Act courageously and you will win more often than you lose. Don't be left wondering 'what if?' years or decades down the track.

* * * * *

Develop a dependable lieutenant that can handle the business in your absence. Such individuals can take a major load from your shoulders and allow you to look at expansion. If your 2IC (second in charge) is very good, you may want to make them a partner in the business so that you don't lose them.

* * * * *

If you are looking for staff and meet high calibre people from other domains in your daily life, offer them a job. The worst thing that can happen is that they say no.

* * * * *

When trying to hire good staff, don't forget to tell potential employees what they will gain - professionally speaking - from working with you. Far too many employers only bother with discussing what *they* want and are actually thrown off balance when a quality candidate asks what the firm will bring to them.

* * * * *

If you are working solo in your small business (which is very common), try to methodically review the previous week's business - you can even use the classic SWOT analysis (Strengths, Weaknesses, Opportunities, Threats). It's easy to lose this reporting perspective on your own but will help keep the project on track and in line with the original vision.

You may even discuss it with your partner - if they're agreeable or masochistic of course.

* * * * *

T hough it can be difficult, try to treat people as though they are where they *could* be - potentially - not where they are at now. This applies to staff and clients. In the process, you will contribute in some way to helping them move towards that potential. This habit is particularly important when people do things that we are unhappy about. It's the principle of the self-fulfilling prophecy applied to your clients and/or staff.

* * * * *

D on't place unrealistic expectations on others, yourself or your business. In the corporate world, the highly toxic ethos of '10% annual economic growth' makes CEOs and CFOs cook the books, bankrupt companies, generally evolve a culture of fiscal deceit and plunder the planet even further. Keep growth and productivity expectations realistic. In fact, a small business' revenue may not grow at all for a year or several years or ever but it may still be viewed as tremendously successful in that it makes you happy, fulfilled and earns enough to comfortably sustain you and your family.

* * * * *

S top talking and just listen. Really listen. It's a habit very few of us have.

* * * * *

T reat everybody with dignity. It's a very rare commodity these days.

* * * * *

Like Henry Ford, make sure that your staff are also some of your customers. This obviously depends on the kind of product or service you offer. But, if your staff can and should be using your business, incentivise them to do so. If staff believe in your business from first hand positive experiences and know exactly how it all works, then how much more convincing will they be when talking to sales prospects?

* * * * *

Interact with the 'small' people at every level of business interaction with the same respect as the top-level brass. Today's secretary is tomorrow's VP.

* * * * *

Always try to remember clients' names, program them into your cellphone and address them by name every time they call. Ask them about an aspect of their life that they told you about another time, e.g. 'How was your trip to Maui in April?'

* * * * *

Print 'one-off' special deals on your invoices even with a graphic image from Microsoft Word's Webdings or Wingdings fonts which the recipient might be interested in. Try to tailor specials highlighted on invoices to each client. If a client or customer is already doing business with you, they are far more likely to expand their business with you than a fresh lead who isn't even aware of your business.

* * * * *

Keep a Word or Excel table up to date every day with income and expenditure. Include all personal and business items down to the cent. The information this gives back is incredible and will immediately reveal where a great deal of money can be saved - especially when projected annually.

* * * * *

Happy staff create a business environment conducive to success. Make sure you avoid hiring people with a negative disposition - they'll find fault in everything. Think of your work culture as an organic entity that will be either positive or negative depending on the 'vibes' that your staff give out. No customer enjoys doing business with lazy, disinterested staff (though they seem to be everywhere!).

* * * * *

If you have a street retail presence, use some form of sandwich board or temporary billboard to promote a 'Deal of the Day' or week to passing traffic. Change it frequently and try to reach different potential customers every time. Remember, you want to entice prospects to trial your business. A killer deal on a selected item is a great way to do it. Don't, however, try to 'bait and switch'. It's illegal and gives prospects a negative taste.

Don't ever let any part of your business stagnate or fall into your mental 'too hard' basket. Whether it's a slow-paying client or a particular part of a store, every area should be lively, managed and properly acknowledged. Think of those shops where a back corner has products covered in dust - such an area influences customers' perceptions about the *whole* store and not just the area.

* * * * *

Instead of increasing revenue (obviously an important goal), try cutting costs e.g. relocating to a cheaper nearby suburb with existing clients, changing your car to a different brand or year if the savings are substantial. It has the same effect as increasing earnings. Big business typically grows profits this way rather than through revenue gain and this is one of the few things we can learn from them.

* * * * *

When staff have worked very hard on a one-off project or big sales period, surprise them with bonus pay or time off.

* * * * *

If talking to a prospect or client and making a promise to contact them within a certain time frame, make sure that you do - even if it is to tell them that you are still working on it for them and will have news soon - such disciplined communication habits mean a lot in a world filled with people who are 'too-busy' to bother. If you think you're too busy to follow up on leads, you'll have plenty of time when there are *no* leads to follow up.

* * * * *

Looking around at how badly other businesses are run is a fantastic education. Just think of how well your business will function just by *not* doing what so many other small and large firms do. Learning what *not* to do is as equally valuable as what to do.

* * * * *

Don't treat your small business like a compromise from what you really want to do with your life. Treat it with passion, enthusiasm, care and time. Your small business should be your *dream* job.

* * * * *

Before making a significant business purchase, ask yourself if leasing is a better option tax-wise, how much extra income the purchase will generate and whether you are buying it because you *want* it or because you *need* it.

* * * * *

Never, ever lose your sense of humour.

* * * * *

Try to lower client expectations then over-deliver rather than the opposite. What you deliver to clients may not vary but their attitude to it will.

* * * * *

Sometimes in business - and life, frankly - it is necessary to contract or shrink in order to expand more formidably later. Never conceive this as failure. While the doors are open for business and you are making money, you are succeeding on some level. But sometimes a temporary contraction is necessary to regroup and fight harder later. Even world champion boxers sometimes have to conserve and evade for a few rounds in a fight rather than swinging non-stop.

* * * * *

Stay on top of tax liabilities. Many small business operators are tempted to cut corners here and later deeply regret it. IRS/taxation staff are not noted for their flexibility or humour.

* * * * *

Enthusiasm and misery are both contagious. Which one are you spreading?

* * * * *

Develop an incredibly professional phone manner and treat all phone enquiries with patience, friendliness and helpfulness. Most businesses today are very poor at handling phone enquiries and consumers are particularly unhappy with the level of service companies give over the phone. 'On hold' times are blowing out more and more. But, if your business makes the phone experience a good one for prospects, you are already *way* ahead of the game.

* * * * *

Occasionally surprise your hardworking staff with rewards and let them know you value their efforts. These cost relatively little - dinners, lunches, chocolates etc - and help sustain long relationships. Everyone likes to feel valued and to have their efforts appreciated. However, avoid overusing this tactic and the bad habit of rewarding 'normal' work performance.

* * * * *

Use the internet to monitor new products, services, tactics and activity in your business area - globally! Do not let any fear or ignorance of computers keep you from harnessing the horsepower of the single greatest research tool in human history.

* * * * *

Give your staff (and yourself) responsibility for mini-projects within the broader 'project' of your small business. That way, it is not just boring, repetitive work but actually has a clearly defined, tangible goal, a 'mission' if you like, for them to get excited about. In fact, a constant series of (finished) mini-projects in your own life – like your own small business! - will help build an interesting life for you. Even offer to be partner or mentor in the development of your staff.

* * * * *

Always conduct a phone conversation in business with both people knowing the name of the person on the other end. If not, stop the call, so that each person is clear on the name of the person they are talking to. This learned technique, routinely done but always with sincerity, always establishes a greater connection between people.

* * * * *

When looking to expand, try to proceed in a manageable, orderly, cautious fashion. Going too big, too soon stretches the resources of the base operation and adds additional stress to all concerned. Aim for incremental growth rather than 'explosive' expansion - the latter may be driven by ego rather than sound business thinking.

* * * * *

Keep exploring ways to refine and streamline your business operations. If, for example, you need to constantly drive a vehicle in your business and continually encounter traffic jams, experiment with different routes or car/public transport communications. Even though I have been involved in business for a long time, I am still discovering little 'silver bullets' that make my work and lifestyle more enjoyable or streamlined. The point is to *keep looking* for such refinements.

Experiment with product names that have the greatest effect. For example, the word 'ultimate' is overused to the point of being meaningless but other superlatives still have some value. The right product or service name can make a big difference.

* * * * *

Don't bother with futile, expensive 'brand-building' advertising - it's the biggest scam in advertising. Instead, use (much cheaper) classifieds or very small display ads to make a concrete, tangible, *finite* offer that your prospect *must* act on to take advantage e.g. free turkey with every quote before Thanksgiving. What better way to build a brand than by having prospects spend money with you and having a good experience in the process? Save your money on 'pretty picture + slogan' advertising – deep down, the marketing world knows it just doesn't work.

* * * * *

Add perceived value to your clients' purchases by giving away something free (or low cost) to you. In adspeak, this is called 'sales promotion' and is applied by everybody from Coca-Cola and McDonalds to the local grocer. Why? Because it works.

* * * * *

View your business from a prospect's point-of-view. Ask yourself, 'would I like it if...?' If there is any doubt, then you need to rectify that aspect of your business.

* * * * *

Instead of providing accounts or credit to clients, encourage them to charge their purchases with you to a credit card. Even if you have to offer a discount to induce this method, credit cards (once authorized) are money in the bank *now* for your business. If that buyer goes under in the future, you will carry *zero* liability because you have already been paid via the credit card charge.

* * * * *

When answering customer complaints, try to handle them yourself or by someone with authority who can act without 'checking with their boss'. Customers get frustrated when a seemingly lowly staff member handles their complaint - someone who has to check about everything. Complaining consumers appreciate fast, friendly, rational and, above all, decisive action by the business. It's actually a good way to turn a potential word-of-mouth 'terrorist' into a 'disciple'.

* * * * *

Always conceive your products or services as solutions to clients' problems - not merely 'things' that you are trying to sell. From their perspective, your sales argument will be far more compelling.

* * * * *

Depending on your business, have free candy/lollies on offer for clients/prospects. Adults have a sweet tooth too!

* * * * *

Keep paperwork properly organized at all times. Never get into the habit of letting papers pile up. Keep everything properly filed and within immediate reach. He or she who has the paperwork always wins. Incoming correspondence - bills etc - should be immediately dealt with and filed where they are grouped and instantly accessible.

* * * * *

When customers/clients do refer your services to others, make sure you acknowledge that kindness and don't give the appearance of taking such a referral for granted.

If staff or yourself go on leave, no client/customer should be left 'hanging' or 'up in the air'. Every client should know exactly what the status of affairs is - even if it is that you are waiting on information/products from another party. Just take the time to let them know when they will be contacted (which is written into a diary of course) before that annual holiday.

* * * * *

Always check spelling on correspondence and marketing materials. Make sure that your e-mail program has the spellchecker turned ON (Outlook Express has this OFF by default; go to Tools-Options-Spelling to fix) and that suspect words or grammar are checked in Word or GoogleDocs.

* * * * *

Your small business should be set up to accept credit cards. Given the ubiquitous nature of 'plastic money' these days, it is inconvenient to expect customers to pay with cash or checks. MasterCard and Visa are must haves though Amex's merchant fees are pretty steep.

* * * * *

Don't be too influenced by fads and trends that you instinctively know are perilous. Look at rising consumer credit card debt, for example. If you have *no* personal/business credit card debt, how much stronger is your financial position than those with $20,000 or $50,000 in debt racked up? Immeasurably! You're Fort Knox by comparison. That kind of debt takes an *awfully* long time to get rid of and most people with such debts seem to have nothing to show for it. It's the same with other fads that are inherently risky. To quote a line from the film, *Ronin*: 'if there's any doubt, then there is no doubt' (i.e. don't do it).

Y ou are not alone. It is estimated that at least 50 million Americans are engaged in a small or home-based business. No matter how grim or lonely you feel at low points in your small business venture/s, many others have been through it and, even better, much of that expertise is available through organizations like the National Association of Home-Based Businesses (www.usahomebusiness.com).

* * * * *

M ake sure that all your insurance bases are covered in your small business. It's fairly troubling to find out *after* a calamity that your insurance didn't cover *that* eventuality with the rogue, runaway Greyhound bus. Talk to insurance companies and small business associations about what *specific* coverage you need.

* * * * *

I f you are dealing with products or services that cost a considerable sum of money, insist on deposits. This action sifts the 'wanna-be' clients from the 'gonna-be's'. If it costs some orders, so be it but it's better than losing the whole cost of an item when the prospect changes their mind. Besides, the deposit will psychologically tie the buyer to the sale. Without it, they don't feel bound and could buy elsewhere.

* * * * *

A lways consult your employees on big decisions, and get their feedback. Your employees are your eyes and ears and they should be explicitly aware of that fact. Therefore by telling them, it will not only in include them into the business 'family', but it may also give them the chance to provide you with some very valuable advice.

* * * * *

Have backup or alternate plans (e.g. a 2nd, cheaper, less powerful computer setup to take over quickly if the main one fails). The more fallback options you have at the 'front end' will save a lot of time, money or hassle at the 'back end'.

* * * * *

Every employee in your operation should be fully aware of the values your business functions by (e.g. all staff treat each other with respect and courtesy, regardless of rank). Nobody will more closely scrutinized more closely on this principle than the owner - you! In terms of your business' values, make sure that you 'walk the walk' as well as 'talking the talk'.

* * * * *

Get into the habit of complimenting staff on one aspect of their work you are happy with. There's no need to make a big ceremony of it, but just a quiet word during an appropriate moment.

* * * * *

Partner with another non-competing business for mutual advantage. Look, for example, how airlines and car rental companies work together. Such arrangements suit both parties and provide natural synergies. The same dynamic can also work on a smaller scale e.g. English tutors and Maths tutors recommending each other to their existing clients.

* * * * *

Review past records of clients or customers who have not used your service/business for some time and do a free and unexpected kindness for them. It won't cost your business much but could re-activate a 'dormant' client.

* * * * *

The best small business operators are always looking to take their operation to 'the next level'. This doesn't mean that they are distracted from the mechanics, tactics and strategies of delivering in the 'here and now' but rather that they are fuelled with the ambition to take it further. This dynamic energises a business in its present condition and doesn't let 'dust' accumulate on the operation.

* * * * *

On random days at the end of trading, ask your staff what was the biggest problem they encountered that day and how it was resolved or needs to be resolved. Fresh observations are very valuable in the refinement of any business. And those morning meetings in the style of *Hill Street Blues* are also very valuable.

* * * * *

Keep all your receipts, and other similar documents. Store them, file them, but never throw them out. The most seemingly irrelevant document today, could be the key piece of evidence tomorrow in a frivolous law suit or tax issue.

* * * * *

Stay on top of new developments in your business field by joining a relevant industry group or groups. Such bodies usually have their 'ear to the ground' and their magazines or newsletters will keep you in touch with new developments in your area - developments that could give you a head start over competitors e.g. Blockbuster managers learning about the emerging threat of movie download services on the Internet.

If your business does accept checks (*not* recommended), make sure that a check verification service is used. These services charge fees of course but are worth it when the alternative is considered. With the number of bogus bank checks around now, every check should be, er, checked!

* * * * *

Use smart people! Bill Gates is no computer whiz, in fact he might not even be that smart. However, he *employs* really smart people with great technical skills in the business. Those people may be smart, but they don't have his entrepreneurial vision.

* * * * *

Always make sure you are getting the best price for your overheads. Shop around, check, bargain and haggle as overheads are usually a hefty proportion of your profit. Even get a staff member to specialize in it as a part of their specified job description. Also evaluate if you actually *need* certain overheads, or if they can be downgraded. For example, does the company car need to be a big gas guzzler, or would a hatchback suffice?

* * * * *

Keep using three words that are in danger of disappearing from the English language: 'please' and 'thank you'.

* * * * *

Eliminate all physical class distinctions between management/you and employees - great businesses have a sense of missionary purpose where everyone is working together towards a common goal. Snobbish staff are better off booted out of your operation so that they can go and work at the local private golf club.

* * * * *

S hake everybody's hand - male or female - and do it often.

* * * * *

A lways legally cover yourself. Don't be afraid to create contracts with employees or colleagues. Any momentary discomfort of overly-legalizing a situation will soon disappear with the piece of mind that all your business secrets and deals are legally protected from being sold to others.

* * * * *

T hrow the marketing jargon handbook in the trash and talk to, and about, people like human beings.

* * * * *

A lways confirm. When you make a plan, deal or transaction, always confirm it at a later date. So if you book a venue for an event, call them a week before the day to make sure everything is running smoothly. If it isn't, you still have time, if you wait for the big day, it could mean disaster. A confirmation call the day before an appointment is a must-do practice.

* * * * *

U nderstand that it is perfectly acceptable for people to disagree on certain issues. Opinions are as changeable and transient as the weather; relationships that matter are not. Keep discussions free of emotion and just stick to the merits of the case. Everyone is entitled to an opinion.

Don't ever air any 'dirty laundry' - either a client's, yours or a staff member's - in front of anyone else. It's totally unprofessional at best and could have unforeseen consequences at worst.

* * * * *

Avoid abusive people. Regardless of what they seem to bring to the table, it will invariably prove to be far less valuable than first appearances suggest. Say no to such individuals - whoever they might be - and move on.

* * * * *

Having a small business challenges us as human beings and in so doing, forces us to develop and realise how much, much more we are capable of than we may have thought. Exciting, huh?

* * * * *

Recognize that having your own small business has less to do with what *job* you have and more to do with your self expression *as a human being*. Your small business is an expression of your aspirational self. Treat it with care.

Opinion is divided on this one but I recommend a pathological hatred of debt. Debt enslaves, cripples and creates a master-slave dynamic that small business operators probably left the corporate sector for in the first place. The irony with debt (mortgages excluded) is that the more of it we have, the less capable we are of paying it back. What a trap! When banks offer 'easy finance', they don't want to give. They want to take. And take.

* * * * *

Be well groomed and dressed at *all* times - it is amazing how many times you will run into clients outside of the professional domain. Professionalism in dress/grooming subconsciously implies professionalism in work habits.

* * * * *

In a new business venture, it may be necessary to appeal to more base human motivations to entice customers or clients into the habit of using your business or service. Greed (perhaps through a desire to save money, for example) can be a powerful lever rather than relying on the longer term, higher level inducements of quality (a clichéd promise that is rarely delivered), relationships and familiarity.

* * * * *

One rule of thumb that business financiers use when evaluating a business loan application is the so called 50/50 rule. In short, they will deduct 50% from the projected income and add 50% to the projected costs. If the venture is still viable, they will proceed to the next round of criteria. Needless to say, few small business plans pass this benchmark.

* * * * *

Continually shop around on bank merchant accounts. Banks view small businesses as lucrative cash cows and charge their fees accordingly. Even if bank fees are tax deductible in your area, they are still a significant drain on the cost of doing business every day. Depending on the business, shopping around on merchant accounts could literally save thousands of dollars a year.

* * * * *

Never lose sight of the fact that it is *profitability* that keeps your business project alive and not merely sales. While sales volume is exciting, the margin involved in those sales must accurately reflect all of the overheads needed in providing that product or service and not just the item itself. Profitability should be monitored on a daily and weekly basis. 20% is generally considered a reasonable net profit on turnover.

* * * * *

Depending on your type of business, it may be possible to sub-let a space within a compatible other business. For example, many counsellors and psychologists use a space within a medical clinic. In so doing, it frees up a great deal of money - especially when calculated annually - that would otherwise be taken up with bond and lease payments.

~

Lightning Source UK Ltd.
Milton Keynes UK
09 March 2010

151135UK00001B/13/P